Addie,
I hope you enjoy this book. I really love you. I want you running with you. to realize how strong you are. you can do anything you put your mind to. Our running going to bring that confidence out of you.

Love,
Daddy

YOUNG RUNNERS AT THE TOP

YOUNG RUNNERS AT THE TOP

A Training, Racing, and Lifestyle Guide for Competitors and Coaches

Brad Hudson
Lize Brittin
Kevin Beck

ROWMAN & LITTLEFIELD
Lanham • Boulder • New York • London

Published by Rowman & Littlefield
A wholly owned subsidary of The Rowman & Littlefield Publishing Group, Inc.
4501 Forbes Boulevard, Suite 200, Lanham, Maryland 20706
www.rowman.com

Unit A, Whitacre Mews, 26-34 Stannary Street, London SE11 4AB

British Library Cataloguing in Publication Information Available

Library of Congress Cataloging-in-Publication Data

Names: Hudson, Brad, author. | Brittin, Lize, 1967– author. | Beck, Kevin, 1969–
   author.
Title: Young Runners at the Top : A Training, Racing, and Lifestyle Guide for
   Competitors and Coaches / Brad Hudson, Lize Brittin, Kevin Beck.
Description: Lanham, Maryland : ROWMAN & LITTLEFIELD, 2017. | Includes
   bibliographical references and index.
Identifiers: LCCN 2016050183 | ISBN 9781442270688 (cloth : alk. paper)
Subjects: LCSH: Running for children. | Running—Training. | Running—Coaching.
Classification: LCC GV1061.18.C45 H84 2017 | DDC 796.42083—dc23 LC record
   available at https://lccn.loc.gov/2016050183

♾TM The paper used in this publication meets the minimum requirements of
American National Standard for Information Sciences—Permanence of Paper
for Printed Library Materials, ANSI/NISO Z39.48-1992.

Printed in the United States of America

CONTENTS

Foreword   vii
    Lize Brittin

Acknowledgments   xi

Introduction   xiii

1   Youth Running in the United States and Abroad   1

2   Body Basics   11

3   Gearing Up   25

4   Running in the Family   33

5   Nutrition for Health and Performance   43

6   The Role of a Mentor   61

7   The Breakdown Lane   69

8   Cross-Training   81

9   Mind Games   93

10   The Club Scene   103

11   Decisions   109

12   Through the Ages   113

Conclusion   125

Bibliography   127

Suggested Resources   129

Index   133

About the Authors   139

FOREWORD

Running is one of the oldest competitive sports known to humankind. It's a curious activity in that it is often challenging, frustrating, and tedious, yet can also be deeply rewarding. Embarking on a running career is like agreeing to take an unprecedented journey, like those of the westward-bound pioneers of early America or the men who first took aim at Antarctica or the summit of Mount Everest; with your first step, you may not know exactly where you'll wind up, but you get the sense that your life will change forever. And it's likely that it will.

Once you start running, chances are good that you will want to continue. Orchestrated correctly, a running career can bring you your happiest, most gratifying moments, and it can also teach you some of the hardest lessons you will ever learn. With running, you face tremendous fears and revel in extraordinary breakthroughs. Through this dizzying range of emotional, mental, and physical experiences, running—in addition to being a way to stay healthy and fit—can become your best friend, a way to cope in a world that's constantly changing. It can be the one constant in your life, and you can learn to love every step, even the heartbreaking ones.

Running allows you to explore your athletic potential and test yourself on every imaginable front. It takes courage to test the bounds of both your mental and physical powers without falling over the edge. One of the biggest flaws in the way young athletes are treated is that they are typically forced to operate on schedules better suited for seasoned adults. They are also not taught how to effectively communicate with their mentors or coaches when something doesn't feel right with their training programs.

In 1983, I set the record at the grueling Pikes Peak Ascent, a half-marathon footrace up a 14,000-foot mountain in Colorado. I was sixteen years old. My running career was just starting, but already I had clocked a 36:17 10K road race at the ever-popular but challenging Bolder Boulder and placed fifth at the Colorado High-School Championships in cross-country. My dreams ranged from winning local road races to making it to the Olympics. During my remaining two years in high school, I was a three-time state cross-country and track champion and twice qualified for the Kinney (now Foot Locker) National Championships, placing seventh as a senior after winning the Midwest Regional meet in Wisconsin, one of four meets nationwide serving as qualifying races for the Nationals. My personal-best 10K time dropped to an impressive 35:04 when I was a senior—at Denver's mile-high altitude, at that. As a freshman in college, I placed second at the Athletics Congress Junior Cross-Country Championships and continued to set records in mountain races around Colorado.

And just as quickly as my rise to success occurred, it crumbled.

Long before I packed my bags and headed off to Utah for my first year of college, despite my manifest success in the sport during high school, I experienced injuries and burnout. I suffered a stress fracture so debilitating I thought I might never run again, and I was under so much pressure, both self-imposed and external, that there were times I wished that this would prove true. Throughout my years in high school, I was also struggling with an eating disorder—anorexia so severe it nearly killed me years later. I endured seizures and extreme panic attacks in my late twenties, but I was eventually able to manage the illness and even recover from it, though this took and continues to take great effort and didn't happen overnight.

None of this is intended as either braggadocio or grousing. The point is that my story is in no way unique. There are countless young, talented athletes who disappear from running before they reach their true potential. Not all of them suffer as greatly as I did, but many live as adults with terrible regrets and the desire to go back and do things differently. Others find ways to accept the paths they chose despite dire consequences. Some—fortunately a small number, but a number that is still too high—don't survive to adulthood at all.

Just when my career was taking off, even as I secretly longed to be free of the intense pressures I had placed on my own shoulders, North Carolina State's Cathy Ormsby, four miles into the 10,000-meter race at the 1986 NCAA Championships in Indiana that she was favored to win, ran off the track at the end of a straightaway, leaped over a fence, and eventually jumped off a bridge onto the banks of the White River. She was left paralyzed due to severe spinal cord injuries. In previous races, Ormsby suffered disturbing panic attacks, and while she can't recall an exact reason why she jumped, she feels a combination of factors contributed to her decision: the physical exertion, the pressure she put on herself, general and performance-related stress, and mental and emotional issues.

I knew on some level that I couldn't bring myself to take such a drastic action, but I understood it fully. Many a time I had longed for the mental and physical rest I couldn't seem to allow myself, and when a more sensible solution doesn't present itself, a drastic one can start to look appealing.

When I was very young, running wasn't something I enjoyed unless I was by myself, not competing. I wasn't very good at it and often came in last place in the sprint-style races held at my elementary school once a year. It wasn't until I was a teen that running turned into something that helped me feel free, confident, and powerful. Once I discovered trail running and could run longer distances, I knew I had found my true passion, and with hard work, I became quite good. In my first two-mile road race, I placed fourth in the women's division. It was clear that I had a natural talent, but I also was dedicated to improving. There were many times that I lined up at the start of a race and felt genuine excitement, and once the gun went off, I remember moments of actual joy running with others. It wasn't until later, after several years of competition, that I started to first fear and then dread running.

One prominent issue I had with running in the early 1980s, when women's running was just starting to flourish (but waif-like Twiggy models still represented the supposedly ideal feminine body type), was that I knew how to handle neither the pressure I was putting on myself nor the sudden attention I was receiving from peers, the media, and the extremely intense and scrutinizing Boulder running community. I felt compelled to push myself as hard as possible both in training and in races, not realizing that this kind of continual stress in the absence of recovery can eventually lead to illness and injury. It can also lead to mental and emotional exhaustion, something I dealt with throughout my entire career.

Fortunately, the body is resilient if given the chance to heal, and often the mind is too. In the aftermath of a running career that ended far too soon, I had to question why someone with such incredible potential wasn't able to realize her long-term goals. There's no doubt that my inability to remain healthy enough to have longevity in the sport wasn't the result of any one thing; it was more the "perfect storm" of factors that truncated not only my career but those of many other young athletes. Looking back, I wish I had learned to enjoy the process of training and racing more instead of focusing exclusively on where I placed or the times I ran. I also wish I had learned at an earlier age that it's okay to do your best and still not win, and that it's also okay to simply "be" and not always have to be accomplishing outstanding feats. At a certain point, running for me became more of a serious, often thankless job than something I did for enjoyment. My entire life and identity was wrapped up in running, and my self-worth hinged on how well I raced. None of this was healthy, and nobody was teaching me to have balance in my life.

Coaches can have a huge impact on a young mind, and as a result, youngsters must be treated with care. Without an open and honest dialogue among coaches, athletes, and parents, a coach can never know if the program he is using is one that's best suited for a given athlete. A coach has to look at athletes as whole people, not just as runners, and has to understand that teams are composed of unique individuals. Not everyone will respond the same way to the same type of training or schedule.

My story doesn't have to be the norm. With an emphasis on providing the right information to coaches and parents, more and better data available on training and nutrition, and strong role models, young athletes can be taught to be outstanding and successful athletes without sacrificing their physical or emotional health. With the proper guidance, young athletes can remain healthy and happy while they reach for their goals, but more importantly, they can adopt a healthy lifestyle that will persist into adulthood and even into old age.

Lize Brittin

ACKNOWLEDGMENTS

Special thanks to contributing writer Addie Bracy. Additional thanks to Bobby McGee, Dr. Richard Hansen, Mark Plaatjes, Lucy and Nerida Alexander, Bean Wrenn, Melody Fairchild, Ruth Waller, Carrie Messner-Vickers, Róisín McGettigan-Dumas, Barb Higgins, Suzy Favor Hamilton, Rebecca Walker, Lorraine Moller, Scott Fry, and Greg Weich.

INTRODUCTION

Young Runners at the Top is an in-depth training guide for young runners of all abilities. At present, there are simply no books in print that combine ways for young runners to become as fast as they can using a long-term approach while providing comprehensive instruction on how to live and think as an athlete and integrate their sport into their academic, family, and social lives.

With special attention to athletes who have excelled both as youngsters and adult athletes, this book takes a look at how young runners can develop the inner strength and discipline required to ensure a long career in a demanding sport—one that, for a variety of reasons, sees myriad Olympic hopefuls as well as everyday recreational runners derailed before they can reach their potential.

The key message of Young Runners at the Top is that it takes the perfect balance of preparation, courage, and health to produce a champion. Having overcome many personal and athletic obstacles in our own lives, we offer specific insight and guidance, whether the reader's goal is to reach the international competitive level or simply enjoy running. We know not only what it takes to become good athletes but also to endure and—above all—maintain a positive attitude and enjoy the act of running for its intrinsic rewards.

No mere assortment of personal highlights and must-dos, this book also includes the wisdom of top coaches, other professional athletes, and even those whose mistakes led them down wrong paths, the latter cautioning others how to avoid errors that can shorten an athletic career. In short, *Young Runners at the Top* offers readers a well-rounded approach to training at any level. It offers comprehensive advice on how they can achieve what might be the most difficult goal in sports for younger athletes: staying sufficiently mentally and physically healthy throughout their development to realize their dreams, whatever those may be.

1

YOUTH RUNNING IN THE UNITED STATES AND ABROAD

Mantra: *Count your blessings*

Kids running for sport and for play is a worldwide phenomenon. Step back from the arena of distance running as a formal, competitive endeavor, and consider what you see when you watch young children scurry and scamper about on a playground, at recess, on a beach, or in their yard. Do you picture them smiling and laughing? Probably so, because children at play are having fun. Running in the modern world is fundamentally more about play than about its primary evolutionary function—raw survival. Play is fun, and fun leads to smiles. No matter what particulars a culture or society may hold, people everywhere want to smile!

THE STATE OF RUNNING IN THE UNITED STATES

It can be discouraging to see running portrayed as something less than fun, enjoyable, or worthy. Children in the 1970s and 1980s lived in an era in which it was routine for gym teachers to punish students for forgetting their gym clothes by having them run laps around the parking lot. It was still the norm for some people to view cross-country and distance events as a refuge for those wanting to be on a "real" sports team but lacking the necessary athletic ability. While runners and running are not nearly as much of a curiosity as was true in our youth—and we'll explore the reasons for this encouraging shift at several points in this text—plenty of people still see it as functionally off-limits, at least to themselves. Too often, the thinking seems to be you're either built for success in running (i.e., whippet-thin) or you're not. Either you can cover ground like an antelope without breaking a sweat, or you should find a better way to expend nervous energy and break a sweat. Believing that you can't be competitive in distance running because you bear little physical resemblance to the East African you just saw win a major marathon is no more reasonable than giving up on basketball because you'll never be 6'9" or abandoning creative writing because none of your first three sonnets or short stories has been compared to the work of Shakespeare.

It is vital for children who are considering running long distances to recognize two things about the sport:

1. No matter who you are and how much talent you have, it is never, ever easy at first. So give it time. It can take a month or several just to feel more comfortable on training runs.
2. Focusing on testing your own limits rather than being concerned with "beating" your fellow runners is a far more sustainable and healthy approach.

As you'd expect, however, factors such as climate, socioeconomic status, and cultural trends combine to dictate the extent to which formal distance running is popular within a particular nation or region. The United States is perhaps the most sports-crazed country on the planet, although our friends in Australia make a strong case for themselves. A sizable portion of our economy relies on competitive sports—shoes, apparel, tickets to events, and both legal and off-the-books betting. Institutions ostensibly established for the purpose of educating young adults dole out millions of dollars a year in "scholarship" money to attendees whose primary and unapologetic mission as "student-athletes" is to make a given varsity athletic team better and thereby raise the university's overall profile and, in some cases, enrich its coffers through enthusiastic alumni giving and cable and network television contracts. The United States is alone in having American-rules football as one of its most avidly watched pastimes, and baseball, basketball, and hockey are considered major-league sports as well. Golf is extremely popular at both professional and amateur levels, and "soccer"—what the rest of the world quite sensibly calls football—has risen steadily in popularity in recent decades. High-schoolers can, in most cases, also choose volleyball, lacrosse, tennis, or wrestling; at private schools, crew (rowing) is another option. Some public schools have varsity swimming, although kids typically compete through nonscholastic club programs (e.g., the YMCA or YWCA).

With all of these games and activities fighting for supremacy, and a colossal premium typically placed on winning, it should come as no surprise that one, distance running remains something of a curiosity to a sizable fraction of the citizenry, and two, that those who take it up and show a modicum of natural talent are often prematurely pushed to their mental and physical limits or otherwise poorly coached. While the number of youth runners is rising, this growth is accompanied by pressure and stress that often causes athletes to burn out at a young age. When examining the training environments of successful athletes, it becomes evident that a fun approach to the sport leads to a longer, more fulfilling career. Coaching methods should emphasize a consistent and gradual progression of development and, most importantly, ensure that the athletes are enjoying what they are doing.

KENYA: LIFESTYLE AND HOPE

Other countries don't share the same competitive intensity toward youth athletes that the United States is known for. When discussing where the world's best distance runners come from, the conversation typically revolves around Kenya, specifically the Kalenjin tribe, made up of about five million people. While it is difficult to identify one single attribute that makes runners from this region so gifted, there are a few factors that stand out as playing a significant role. Most researchers would agree that biological makeup and socioeconomic factors are largely responsible for the talent that is cultivated there. However, you can't discuss athletes from this region without mentioning that most of them grew up running. With kids often having to run several miles to and from school or into town, the activity is most often seen as a mode of transportation, not exercise. Additionally, Kenya is a very poor country offering very few job opportunities outside of farming and almost no secondary schools. Many young runners from this region view the sport as a financial opportunity rather than an obligation or even a sport. Running can provide young Kenyans with an escape from poverty, and their relationship with it is often one built on hope for a future.

SOUTH AFRICA: FITNESS VS. FEROCITY

Former world marathon champion Mark Plaatjes experienced the difference in youth sports firsthand when he came to the United States from South Africa on a running scholarship. During his time as an athlete in

South Africa, there was less pressure placed on winning and more emphasis placed on having fun. The high-school program in which he participated in South Africa was one that focused on building aerobic capacity first with very little speed work. He and his high-school teammates would run hills and endurance runs during the week and only occasionally step on the track for intervals, but long before participating in an organized running program, he was developing his endurance and increasing his strength simply because his lifestyle was one that included a lot of activity: walking to school, playing soccer, and general play after school.

When Plaatjes made the move to the United States, he noticed a priority shift, and his career suffered. Feeling the pressure to win every race and with very little focus on long-term development, Plaatjes experienced injuries and decreased satisfaction with running. After talking to his coach and expressing his concerns, they were able to adjust the training and racing environment to create a more sustainable and successful approach, one that drew on his experiences running in his home country. He went on to log a long and successful career before eventually retiring and beginning a career as a physical therapist.

Now living and working in Boulder, Colorado, Plaatjes treats some of the area's best athletes, including youth runners. When he started his practice almost twenty-eight years ago, only about 5 percent of his patients who came to him with injuries were kids. Now Plaatjes estimates that number has increased to almost 40 percent. He believes this rise in numbers can be attributed to a youth training environment that is too competitive and the fact that there is no real off-season. Young athletes who train with peers the majority of the time are more likely to push their bodies too hard and neglect rest and recovery. Kids should be encouraged to take it easy when they are feeling the toils of hard training rather than push through pain and discomfort to stick with their teammates. Plaatjes also believes that in the United States, there is no clearly defined off-season that can be completely dedicated to resting. Instead, coaches and athletes try to peak all year long, a tactic that is not sustainable over the long term.

THE UNITED STATES: POLARIZATION IN ACTION

As a renowned running coach and former professional runner, Brad Hudson has a slightly different story. As a young runner, he logged almost unheard-of mileage for an athlete his age. However, his motivation and desire to do so was his own and was not catalyzed by a parent or coach. He loved running and used it as an escape from some of the chaos surrounding his family life. While he trained that way himself, Brad does not recommend the same level of intensity for a typical young long-distance runner. The risk of injury is too high. He states that one of the major differences between youth athletes in the United States and those in other countries is that the latter are generally more active. In other countries, kids tend to spend more time playing outdoors, running to and from school, and engaging in other sports and activities.

One exception to this worldwide pattern is Japan, where runners might specialize, compete, and accumulate more mileage at an earlier age, but the younger athletes are well taken care of by a team of individuals including coaches, dietitians, physical therapists, and mentors. They also tend to do a lot of walking or cross-training during their off-season and build a very solid aerobic base before working on speed or racing. Importantly, they don't face the grind of collegiate competition, as virtually all successful American and Canadian athletes do.

Brad notes that in the United States, we see young people standing at extremes of the fitness spectrum, with some kids being highly active in competitive sports and others essentially doing nothing in the way of physical activity. Some kids are very fit and are pushed very hard in their sport, and then there are those who spend most of their time in front of the computer screen or TV. Brad feels that Americans tend to be too performance-oriented and that it is better to promote general fitness to younger athletes and let them develop over the long term at their own rate. In the United States, we see more burnout, a term that refers to both short-term and possibly long-term physical and mental exhaustion, because youth athletes are pushed too hard early on rather than being taught how to achieve both emotional and physical longevity in the sport.

AUSTRALIA: A BALANCING ACT

For eleven-year-old Lucy Alexander, a successful Australian distance runner who has hopes of qualifying for Nationals in track or cross-country one day, putting her energy into other activities such as swimming and horseback riding in addition to running helps keep her balanced and healthy. Her training schedule allows her complete days away from running, even though running is the sport where she finds the most success. It's a fine line between doing too much too soon and not doing enough to reach both short- and long-term goals, so Lucy has to be aware of the best way to train for herself. For example, in order to reduce the risk of injury, she makes sure to do her longer runs on soft surfaces, something we recommend for all runners, young and old. Swimming two times a week also gives her legs a rest from the pounding of running.

Lucy admits that there are times when she doesn't like training, but she loves pushing herself and seeing the results of her hard work. For her, the gratification from doing well is what motivates her to keep at it on days when she's having a harder time feeling excited about lacing up her running shoes and getting out the door. She also trains with either a coach or her father, a professional triathlete, and others who are more experienced because being social while training can decrease any self-imposed pressures and keep her from doing too much before she is ready.

NEW ZEALAND: EFFORT AS ITS OWN REWARD

To four-time Olympian Lorraine Moller, the United States' approach to youth sports is glaringly different than that of her native New Zealand. When referring to competing in her youth, Moller says that growing up in New Zealand, the focus wasn't on winning. Kids competed in fun runs and people raced, but everyone was celebrated. It's not so much that everyone got a ribbon for participating but that everyone was recognized for putting in hard effort. The point of the race isn't to win but more to challenge yourself. She goes on to point out that coaches and parents in the United States place way too much emphasis on performance results. While it is important to reward and recognize athletes who are performing well, this should not be done at the expense of those in the middle or at the back of the pack. Participation, commitment, and work ethic should always be celebrated and stressed regardless of the outcome of the race. Many European countries share this kind of lifestyle when it comes to running.

THE COACH'S ROLE

With American runners recently becoming more competitive on the international stage, more athletes are targeted when showing promise at a young age and are being placed in strenuous training programs before they are even physically mature. It is not uncommon for a very talented high-school athlete to break out into the national scene and then become somewhat unknown a few years later as the result of both physical and mental burnout. Much of this problem can be mitigated by having a clear idea of what the coach's role should be and how they define success. Coaching success should be identified based on low attrition and the development of athletes rather than on optimizing a young runner's performance for one or two years at the expense of a long-term career. Unfortunately, coaches are often under pressure to get results and end up focusing more on race outcomes than on the well-being of individual athletes.

Richey Hansen, a chiropractor, physical therapist, and running coach in Boulder, attributes many of the issues in American youth running to the lack of proper education within that demographic. A former middle-school and high-school coach with an educational background in exercise physiology, Hansen identifies the certification and testing procedures necessary to become a mentor at that level as not being comprehensive. The USA Track and Field high-school certification process leaves potential coaches unprepared for how to put concepts together to form successful, long-term plans for their athletes. Instead, those in charge of training young athletes create intense training schedules and prioritize peaking for state meets several times a year, losing sight of the fact that many of the athletes are still developing physically, mentally, and emotionally. Hansen says that the role of a coach should not be to optimize students' potential while in one limited cross-country or track season; it's more to look at what will help the athlete form a forward-looking perspective, both mentally and structurally, and stay interested and active in the sport over the long term.

These typical performance-based programs don't allow for phases of training or periodization. Creating a training plan that includes different phases in one cycle with a rest period after the cycle produces stronger and better-adjusted athletes. Most athletes not only benefit from this kind of training, but they also find the variety in each phase of training more enjoyable than doing the same kind of training year-round.

Typically, a base phase or building phase of easy running is followed by a preparation phase that includes tempo runs and a modicum of speed work. The last phase, or the peak phase, is designed to simulate racing, with faster workouts and intervals added. A rest phase is as essential as the other phases, and this is something that is often lacking in programs that go from seasons of cross-country to indoor track to outdoor track and then road racing or more track racing during the summer. The length of each stage can vary, but each phase has specific types of exercises that build on those in the previous phase. It's easier to set specific goals for each phase, and athletes are less likely to fall into overtraining or suffer burnout when following this kind of plan.

Young athletes develop at different rates. Being in charge of a high-school team can mean advising athletes ranging from fourteen years old to eighteen years old. While this is "only" a four-year spread, the upshot is vast differences in physical development, with each athlete manifesting very different capabilities. A coach must be able to discern the needs of each individual runner and determine what approach will be most beneficial for them. When working with young athletes, there is no "one size fits all" approach, and a good coach must be intuitive enough to recognize what each athlete needs to be successful, healthy, and happy.

HOW YOUNG IS TOO YOUNG?

A major concern for many coaches and parents is determining what age is appropriate for their child to start running. Additionally, once an athlete has found his or her way into the sport, his or her advisers must ponder what type of volume and intensity load the children can handle.

Unfortunately, there is no single right answer to these important questions. Kids tend to grow and mature at very different rates. What may be an appropriate training load for one child of a given age may be completely different from that of another child of the same age. One of the best ways to monitor these two issues—volume and intensity—is to simply listen to the athlete. Very young kids should not be forced to run. If they show an enthusiasm for doing so, that should be fostered and encouraged. However, if their attitude and demeanor suggest that they are fatigued or experiencing pressure to perform, their training should be reduced.

Brad notes that the younger an athlete is, the more time he or she should spend doing things other than steady running. Ireland's Róisín McGettigan-Dumas, a 2008 Olympian in the 3,000-meter steeplechase, agrees. Having spent much of her childhood in Ireland participating in many different sports, she was able to enjoy being a part of running clubs but didn't focus specifically on running until she was fifteen years old. Róisín moved to the United States several years later to attend college. As a result, she was able to develop at an appropriate rate, remaining interested in running and staying physically sound enough to qualify for the Beijing Olympics in 2008. She feels that problems arise when an athlete becomes too identified with her sport and becomes overly serious, leaving no room for fun. Róisín was fortunate that her coaches were able to help her set and achieve her goals while making sure she didn't lose her identity as a person or lose sight of enjoying her sport, even at the elite level.

Like Róisín, Ruth Waller enjoyed participating in many different sports and being in the outdoors. She grew up in Manchester, England, a place she feels is more laid-back when it comes to running. While she did join a running club and begin competing when she was eleven years old, she notes that English people in general tend to run for fun and because they enjoy it. As a result, she and her peers often make their sport a lifelong habit. When Ruth moved to the United States, she noticed that kids are made to specialize early and are pushed to a higher level at too young an age. Their overall mileage is much higher than what Ruth remembers she and her peers attempting. This increased mileage and intense focus are often at odds with promoting longevity in the sport.

Athletes don't develop into great runners just from starting to log miles at a young age. Brad recommends incorporating coordination and agility drills as a supplement to running for the younger age groups. He believes that doing so helps create a solid foundation for handling more training down the road, and participating in other activities such as gymnastics and soccer can be a great way to have fun while building overall athletic capacity. Runners who aren't fully developed are dealing with a very different physiological profile than those who have been in the sport for a while. This difference is one that must be not only recognized but accommodated. As the athlete gets older and accumulates more years of training, the workload can be increased. This progression should be managed gradually and intelligently and rely strongly on feedback from the athlete.

No matter what their country of origin, young athletes exude an enthusiasm for competition and sport. There are many things to be gained from participating in athletics as a kid, particularly cross-country and track and field. When accompanied with the right guidance from both coaches and parents, youth runners can experience success while ensuring that they will be able to physically and mentally enjoy the activity for many years to come. By placing the emphasis on finding joy in the most basic form of human movement and seeking the rewards of hard work and commitment, you, as a mentor, will create an environment conducive to success in every sense of the word.

2

BODY BASICS

Mantra: *I am strong*

Running changes people's bodies. This can happen in ways that are obvious to others, as when a formerly sedentary person loses weight after getting active. But the changes we are most concerned with in this chapter are the physiological adaptations and stresses that occur in young people at cellular and musculoskeletal levels—factors that are of special concern in bodies that are naturally growing and maturing in ways independent of exercise, as those of children, teenagers, and young adults are.

One of the most important things to remember when working with young athletes is that their bodies are still developing. *They cannot be merely seen as younger versions of adult athletes.* Their bodies are physiologically in a very different place from those of their elders, and those differences must be accounted for in order to be successful in keeping young athletes safe from injury and potential long-term damage. Every athlete matures at a different rate, implying that each individual has a different workload-handling capacity. Prescribing too many miles or too much intensity to a young runner can lead to injuries and physical damage, in some cases permanent ones.

ATHLETE MATURATION

The period in which children typically experience their biggest adolescent growth spurt is between twelve and fifteen years old for females and fourteen to seventeen years old for males. This phase is usually accompanied by wide variations in athletic ability, motor coordination, physical development, and skill sets. Each athlete will move along at a different pace. From early childhood to full maturation, kids will work their way through pre-puberty, puberty, post-puberty, and finally full maturation. Each of these stages includes its own unique set of characteristics that will affect kids and teens as athletes. As a coach, it is important to know roughly where each athlete stands along the path of maturation so as to account for the effect that a particular type of training will have.

THE LTAD MODEL

Presented by Istvan Balyi in the 1990s and further developed and explored in later years, the Long-Term Athlete Development (LTAD) model includes seven stages designed to help coaches responsibly develop young athletes. These stages are Active Start (0–6 years), FUNdamentals (girls 6–8, boys 6–9), Learn to Train (girls 8–11, boys 9–12), Train to Train (girls 11–15, boys 12–16), Train to Compete (girls 15–21, boys 16–23), Train to Win (girls 18+, boys 19+), and Active for Life (any age). The first three stages of this model are designed to build basic skills before puberty to prepare children to be active for the rest of their lives. The best way to do this is to make sure kids are having fun while moving and ensure that they are learning good habits around physical activity. Stages 4 through 6 focus on high-level training for young athletes wanting to specialize in a specific sport. Kids will develop endurance and more specific skills associated with the sport or sports of their choice in these phases. The seventh and final stage is intended to keep young adults generally active and fit for the rest of their lives.

The LTAD model identifies and focuses on ten key elements:

- *Physical Literacy*. This relates to the ability to move with ease, confidence, and control in a variety of situations. In other words, the athlete is able to assess a given situation and the environment and apply the appropriate skill set of greatest benefit to himself or herself and those nearby. This includes using proper judgment, having the ability to read the surrounding environment, and developing sound decision-making skills.
- *Specialization*. This refers to a focus on one activity. Certain sports, such as ballet, gymnastics, and figure skating, require early specialization in order to reach peak performance at an age that would allow

for success in competition at the national or international level. Most sports are late-specialization sports; however, all sports and athletes should be individually analyzed to determine whether early specialization is a reasonable option. An intense focus on one sport at too early an age can actually hinder later performance if physical literacy has not been achieved first.

- *Developmental Age.* Growth, development, and rate of maturation are the result of many factors. Each child is affected by genes, hormones, nutrients, and the environment, and the interactions of each of these affect individual children differently and at different chronological ages. As a result, each child will grow and develop at different rates. The differences are not as pronounced after the age of twenty or thereabouts.
- *Sensitive Periods.* In general, it's better to err on the side of undertraining rather than overtraining. That said, learning specific skills and building the foundation for a specific sport is particularly effective during a certain time frame. Sensitive periods address the trainability of an athlete during times when the body is more responsive and adapts more effectively to training stimuli.
- *Mental, Cognitive, and Emotional Development.* Training encompasses more than physical and technical skills. There is also a psychological aspect to performance that requires development. This includes mental skills, emotional regulation, ethical sportsmanship, and sound decision making.
- *Periodization.* Periodization is a method of training that provides athletes with long-term structure and a basic outline to follow. This outline includes both long- and short-term goals and breaks down training sessions into phases lasting weeks or months, each specific to developing certain aspects of skill or fitness. An overview of training should include individual sessions, daily activities, and weekly activities and monthly sessions, with everything from volume, frequency, and intensity of training, as well as recovery and rest, included.
- *Competition.* For very young athletes, the focus should always be more on physical development than on competition. As an athlete matures, goals pertaining to competition can be formulated and implemented. Even at an elite level, when the focus is chiefly on competing, an athlete should never lose sight of enjoying the process and staying physically healthy.
- *Excellence Takes Time.* How long it takes a given athlete to reach his highest level of achievement depends on the characteristics of the individual. There's no doubt that excellence takes time, probably years

of practice for most, but there will never be one grand plan or "golden rule" in terms of how to reach the peak performance. In the sport of running and other physically demanding activities, the athlete has to train wisely, not necessarily more, in order to achieve success. Though there are many different ways to train, one universal truism is that reaching excellence takes time and a lot of hard work.

- *System Alignment and Integration.* No matter the sport in which an athlete participates, system alignment and integration suggests that all teams, clubs, individuals, and coaches come together for the betterment of the sport. While building better athletes is a worthy goal, creating a better local, regional, or national sports system is equally important. The more the community at large gets involved, the better everything becomes for both individuals and large groups in the sport. A sense of camaraderie will encourage everyone who participates, from coaches to athletes to spectators.

- *Continuous Improvement.* The last element is one that addresses continuous improvement. One must always be willing to look at emerging developments and information in order to keep striving for the best practices in coaching and development. Coaching styles and programs should be flexible and evolve in order to provide the most up-to-date instruction. Breakthroughs in sports science research cannot be ignored when it comes to coaching practices, and coaches should be willing to incorporate new ideas into an existing program if they show promise in terms of being useful to athletes.

These ten factors outline important areas of human development in the context of athletics and must be monitored by coaches and parents to ensure long-term success in running and other sports.

AVOID MONOTONY

Even athletes who show tremendous promise as runners from a young age should be encouraged to engage in many different sports and activities. Suggesting that young runners only participate in cross-country or track and field not only increases their chances of injury, but, paradoxical though it may seem, may ultimately reduce their potential as runners. *The younger the athlete, the less time she should spend actually running.* Until an athlete is at least, say, ten to twelve years old, formal or regular running should be largely avoided, especially programmed intense running. Early on, running should be incorporated as part of play or games. For very young children, games like tag, relay races, and soccer will help build agility, endurance, and strength. If a coach is intent on implementing formal training, running should be broken up with drills and other movements that differ from running.

As young athletes age and their bodies start to mature, more running can be added to the mix. However, during any stage of training, it is beneficial to continue agility and coordination drills, form work, and plyometrics. Prescribing this type of training to your athletes will help instill proper biomechanics and efficient movement while their bodies are still developing, creating the foundation for a healthier, more durable athlete down the road. As always, working hard doesn't imply a lack of genuine fun. On the contrary, working on drills in teams of two or in a relay are ways to keep the hard work more entertaining and engaging.

BONE DEVELOPMENT

Between the approximate ages of nine and twelve, kids often begin a physical growth spurt or at a minimum begin growing at a faster rate than before. During this time, the bones in young athletes' legs begin to grow more quickly. In this early stage of development, the bones lack ossification, or complete hardening. Running too much or too often can place the body under a high level of stress, causing aches and pains that may progress to serious medical conditions. Because most of the growth occurs at the developing cartilage located at the ends of bones, the joints are especially susceptible to pain or injury. As athletes move into their early teen years, they tend to experience accelerated overall body growth without yet having bones that are completely mineralized. Adding too much volume to their training program raises the risk of stress reactions or stress fractures, the former often being a step along the way to the latter.

In young children, bones develop as small fragments of old bone are replaced by new bone. Since bone is living, vascularized tissue, its structure will change and become longer and denser as a child develops. Proper nutrition that includes ample vitamin D and calcium is essential to encourage new bony deposits that eventually form permanent bone. In addition to the central bone growing, there are growth plates at the ends of each bone that determine the length of the bone in an adult. Once the bone is fully mature, these cartilaginous plates close and are replaced by actual bone. Since the plates are softer than bone, these locations are where injuries are highly likely to develop in a young athlete. Whereas an adult might sustain a slight strain or sprain in the joint as the result of overtraining or trauma, a child is likely to develop an actual fracture of the growth plate. Soft tissue reacts differently in children as well, and even if the growth plate is not affected, sprains, strains, and other injuries commonly occur.

DEVELOP OVERALL STRENGTH

During all stages of growth and body maturation, kids are getting taller and longer without first developing the muscular strength to support their burgeoning infrastructure. One of the most common mistakes youth running coaches make is not recognizing this fact and increasing their athletes' running volume while ignoring general strength training. (A lack of adequate strength training, in fact, persists among runners of all ages.) If a coach spends time helping young runners develop the muscle mass necessary to be stronger, more coordinated athletes, her runners are more likely to be successful and healthy in both their short-term and long-term careers.

There are a number of advantages to incorporating some kind of weight or strength program into young athletes' training. The primary reason is to reduce the risk of injuries, but an overall stronger body will perform better, too. Structural fitness refers to the ability of a developing child's bones, ligaments, muscles, and tendons to tolerate the impact of running without incurring damage. With as little as fifteen minutes of strength training a day, runners can reduce their chances of getting injured, and in a sport that unfortunately features some of the highest injury rates, building strength is not merely wise, but necessary.

FEMALE DEVELOPMENT

Adolescence and puberty are a very challenging time for female athletes. Their bodies are going through many hormonal and developmental changes. The physiological changes that young girls experience during puberty can often cause running to be difficult and even feel unnatural. It is natural for young women to gain weight during this time of physical development. Often, girls choose to fight these changes, and this can lead to injuries and malnourishment.

The *female athlete triad*, though an incomplete method of measuring overall health and wellness, is still a very important concept to bear in mind when working with young girls. An athlete suffering from this condition has *absent or irregular menstrual cycles, low bone density,* and *potentially disordered eating.* Left untreated, these issues not only lead to injuries such as stress fractures but can also cause more serious problems later in life, including infertility and early osteoporosis. In severe cases, an eating disorder can cause death. As they begin to gain weight—a natural part of maturing as a young woman—female athletes sometimes neglect the nutrition their bodies need in their efforts to lose weight.

Losing weight is tempting because girls who see elite runners often focus on the thinnest athletes they see while ignoring counterexamples and believe that they need to emulate this body type in order to be maximally successful. From a numbers standpoint, a lower body mass does indeed translate to a higher VO2Max, which entails a higher level of oxygen utilization. (VO2Max is defined as milliliters of O_2 used per minute, per kg of body weight.) There is a trade-off, however, and a body that's too lean can't perform to its theoretical potential. In addition, a low body-fat percentage combined with high levels of activity can decrease estrogen levels and cause amenorrhea (a cessation of menstruation) or irregular menstrual cycles. As a result, bone density may diminish, increasing the risk of osteoporosis or bone-related injuries. Any bone density lost during this very important stage of development can never be regained, reinforcing the importance of coaches' awareness of this serious condition. It is crucial that coaches and parents help athletes develop good eating and nutritional habits early on. It is also important that a coach be willing to adjust a runner's training to work around hormonal fatigue and cycles.

Overtraining, especially in young women, is virtually guaranteed to interfere with an athlete's hormonal homeostasis. This can lead to symptoms such as chronic fatigue, restlessness, poor recovery, excessive muscle soreness, general fatigue, an elevated heart rate, and sleeplessness. Replacing some running with resistance training while properly nourishing the body can help raise lowered levels of hormones such as testosterone and human growth hormone to healthy ranges. This will certainly make the athlete feel better and is clearly the route to optimal health.

None of this is intended to imply that youngsters or young girls shouldn't run or compete. It's perfectly fine for kids to ramble about and even run long distances. Still, great care should be taken to make sure children engage in activity in a way that's healthy and enjoyable. Just because a child can do something doesn't mean she should. The ultimate goal isn't to accumulate as many miles as possible; it's to build strong, able bodies. You only get one body in life, so coaches and parents should make sure that the children they mentor don't reach adulthood tired and broken. The aim is to help the athlete arrive at the next stage of life in good working order, whether that stage includes competing, recreational activities, or something less intense.

SAMPLE SCHEDULES

Keeping in mind that each runner is unique and will be able to handle different workloads at different ages and different stages of development, we are well aware of the kind of training kids, especially those in high school, are doing in the United States in order to compete at a national level. We strongly caution coaches to look at each runner as an individual and assess what each child can handle training-wise. Not every child will be able to run long distances and emotionally or physically handle the intensity of competition and what others can more easily manage. As a cautionary note, "Brad's Advanced Program" schedules are designed for those who are already dedicated to the sport and have goals of competing at a top level, just to give others an idea of the kind of training that some kids are capable of successfully carrying out at the end of a competitive season. These kinds of schedules are not designed to be followed year-round. When done cautiously and with personalized guidance from the coach and feedback from the athlete, though, these kinds of tough schedules can produce outstanding results during the competitive season.

Brad insists that the focus in even the most challenging schedules for younger athletes should be on building an aerobic base and teaching the fundamentals of running. In order to promote longevity in the sport, Brad creates advanced programs that are not highly focused on fast or interval running.

One aspect of training that Brad strongly stresses is making sure that recovery days truly remain as such. Another consideration is the general schedule of the athlete. School, family events, and important social relationships and engagements must be balanced with any running schedule.

For ages five to nine years old, Brad suggests running barefoot when and where possible. Most drills should be done over a flat, soft surface of about ten meters. Drills for all ages include:

1. Forward Arm Circles: This is a walking or skipping drill. While walking or skipping forward, rotate both arms in a wide, forward motion like a windmill.
2. Backward Arm Circles: This is a walking or skipping drill. While walking or skipping forward, rotate both arms in a wide, backward motion like a windmill.
3. Side-Skip Arm Circles: This is a skipping drill. Facing one direction, sashay while bringing your arms up over your head and back down, so that each arm is completing a half circle. Make sure to face the opposite direction, so that each leg has a chance to lead.

4. Ninja: While walking or jogging forward, straighten one leg out straight while reaching toward it with the opposite hand. Alternate legs every couple of steps.

5. A-Skip: This is an exaggerated skip. While skipping forward, bring your knees up high on each step, making sure your arms are in sync with the exaggerated motion of your legs.

6. B-Skip: Start an A-skip, but while your knee is high in the air, kick your lower leg out straight and quickly drive it to the ground, pulling it underneath you every few strides.

7. High Knees: This is a running drill. Be sure to lean forward slightly as you jog forward and bring your knee up high with each stride. Pump your arms in sync with your legs as you do this drill.

8. Butt Kicks: This is a running drill. Lean forward slightly. As you jog forward, bring your heel toward your glutes, exaggerating your back kick every few strides.

9. Combo A-Skips: This is a running drill. As you jog forward, bring one leg up and quickly back down in a similar motion to the B-skip. Alternate legs every few strides.

10. Fast-Leg Butt Kicks: This is a faster version of regular butt kicks. Instead of bringing your heel to your glutes every few steps, bring it up every stride.

11. Fast-Leg B-Skips: This is a faster version of the B-skip. Instead of bringing your leg up and quickly back down every few strides, do this every stride.

12. Karaoke or Grapevines: This is a sideways drill. Start facing one direction. Raise your arms up, so that they are parallel to the ground. Start out walking and move into a jog as you step sideways, first lifting your right foot over your left, twisting your body as needed. Follow through by bringing your left foot around back to the starting position and, on the next step, placing your right foot behind your left. Be sure to do both sides.

13. Side Shuffle: This is a sideways drill. Squat slightly with your hands on your hips. Facing one direction, sashay, holding the form. Turn around and do the drills in the opposite direction.

14. Crossovers: This is a sideways run. Start facing one direction. Your right foot will be continually crossing in front of your left as you move sideways, crossing over with each step. Be sure to do both sides.

AGES FIVE TO NINE

Beginner

Day 1	Day 2	Day 3	Day 4	Day 5	Day 6	Day 7
15-minute easy run with Mom or Dad; informal drills	Off OR outside play OR swimming with friends	1/2-mile warm-up + 6 strides on the infield of a track or on the grass + 1/4-mile cooldown	10-minute energetic WALK + pick 4–6 drills to do that are not the same as on Day 1	Off OR outside play OR swimming with friends	30 minutes of running GAMES such as tag or soccer OR 1/4-mile warm-up followed by 1-mile time trial + walk 1/4 mile to cool down	3-mile hike (not running) with family OR a family bike ride of 5 miles with rest stops as needed

Intermediate

Day 1	Day 2	Day 3	Day 4	Day 5	Day 6	Day 7
10–15-minute run + five 10-second strides + pick 4 drills	Off OR soccer, swimming, playing on the playground, or other active sport	10-minute run + 4x 60m strides + pick 6 drills + 1/4-mile cooldown	Off OR swimming with friends	15–20 minutes of easy fartlek running in a grassy park with at least one hill OR create a scavenger hunt	Soccer or alternative activity	3–5-mile hike OR walk with 10 random 30-second stretches of running
	10 minutes of stretching or yoga (optional)		10 minutes of stretching or yoga (optional)			

Brad's Advanced Program

Day 1	Day 2	Day 3	Day 4	Day 5	Day 6	Day 7
20-minute run + drills	Soccer, swimming, basketball, gymnastics, dance, or other active sport + agility and core work for 20 minutes	20–25 minutes of running + drills + 6x 60m flyers	Soccer, swimming, basketball, gymnastics, dance, or other active sport + 10–20 minutes of yoga or core work	20–25 minutes running + drills + 6x 60m flyers + 6x one-legged jumps	Soccer, swimming, basketball, gymnastics, dance, or other active sport + 10–20 minutes of yoga or core work	10-km hike/jog OR combination on soft surfaces

AGES TEN TO THIRTEEN

Beginner

Day 1	Day 2	Day 3	Day 4	Day 5	Day 6	Day 7
2 miles easy run + pick 4 drills	1 hour swimming, biking, or active games with friends	1.5 miles + 4x 100m strides + pick 6 drills + 1/4-mile cooldown	Off OR 15–20 minutes of yoga or stretching	See Day 2 OR 1 mile warm-up + pick 4 drills + 4x 50m of skipping + 1/4-mile cooldown	5-km race OR 4-mile run on the trails	3–5-mile hike OR 8-mile bike ride

Intermediate

Day 1	Day 2	Day 3	Day 4	Day 5	Day 6	Day 7
2–3 miles easy run + pick 6 drills	1 hour swimming, soccer, or other active sport	Warm up 10 minutes + 2 miles of fartlek OR tempo running + 1/4-mile cooldown	Off OR leisure swimming, biking, or active games with friends	1.5-mile run + drills + 4x 50m skipping + 1/4-mile cooldown	3-km cross-country race OR a hilly fartlek session of 20–25 minutes after a warm-up	10-km hike OR cross-training day

Brad's Advanced Program

Day 1	Day 2	Day 3	Day 4	Day 5	Day 6	Day 7
8–10-km run + drills + 10 short hills (10–12 second) + 6 one-footed jumps on each foot	1–2 hours of activity that can include: gymnastics, basketball, soccer, swimming, field hockey, ice hockey, or any other aerobic sport	8–10-km run + drills + 6x 60m flyers (strides) + 8x one-footed jumps	1–2 hours of activity (see Day 2) + 20 minutes of core work, yoga, or Pilates	8–10-km run + drills + 8x 60m flyers + 6x one-footed jumps	Alternative activities such as soccer, biking, swimming, gymnastics, etc.	15-km run OR hike OR a combination on the trails or a soft surface

AGES FOURTEEN TO SEVENTEEN

Beginner

Day 1	Day 2	Day 3	Day 4	Day 5	Day 6	Day 7
Warm up 2 miles + 8x 400m at race pace with 400m jog between + 1-mile cooldown	4 miles very easy OR cross-train	Warm up 10 minutes + 30 minutes of easy fartlek + pick at least 6 drills + 5-minute cooldown	4 miles very easy OR cross-train	3 miles very easy + pick at least 6 drills	5-km race	5 miles very easy run OR hike/jog combination of 6 miles total
	10–15 minutes of yoga or core work		10–15 minutes of yoga or core work			

Intermediate

Day 1	Day 2	Day 3	Day 4	Day 5	Day 6	Day 7
Warm up 2 miles + 6x 800m at just below race pace with full rest between + 1-mile cooldown	A.M.: 2-mile run + 6–8 drills	20-minute warm-up + 6–8x 1-minute hill climbs at TEMPO (not race) pace, jogging between each + 10–15-minute cooldown	A.M.: 3-mile run + 10–15 minutes of core or yoga/stretching	Easy 4-mile run on the grass OR cross-train for 40 minutes	Warm-up + 5-km time trial or race OR 25 minutes of fartlek	Very easy recovery run or hike of 7 miles
	P.M.: 3-mile run + 10–15 minutes of core or yoga/stretching		P.M.: 2-mile run + 6–8 drills + 4 10-second strides	Relaxing swim or short walk		

Brad's Advanced Program

Day 1	Day 2	Day 3	Day 4	Day 5	Day 6	Day 7
A.M.: 8-km easy run	8-km run OR cross-train 25 minutes	15–20-km run + 20 minutes of core work	8-km run OR cross-train 25 minutes	8-km run OR off	Race 5 km or 10 km	15–20-km recovery run
P.M.: 10 km easy + 8–10 short (about 10–12 seconds) hill repeats + core work	P.M.: 3km warm-up + drills + 34 minutes fartlek (repeat 1,2,3,2,1,2,3,2,1 minutes with equal rest) + short warmdown + strength training/plyometrics		5-km run + drills + 4–6x 1600m threshold + 6x 60m flyers + 3-km cooldown run + strength training/plyometrics	Easy 8–10km run + 4–6x 60m barefoot strides on grass		

3

GEARING UP

Mantra: *I move forward with confidence*

One of the most appealing aspects of running is that, unique among popular sports, it doesn't require much equipment. No matter where you are in the world, you can usually get out and go for a run.

The sport doesn't always favor those with access to advanced resources. All you really need are a good pair of running shoes and proper workout attire.

When Kevin and Brad were teenagers in the 1980s, about the most sophisticated way—the only way, really—for most people to determine the length of a run was using a car odometer. As Kevin started taking to the New Hampshire woods for longer and longer trail runs, where using a car to measure distances was obviously out of the question, he came up with a way to estimate how far he was running. Using his grandfather's U.S. Geological Survey topographical maps, which usually showed major trails as dotted lines, he would hold a length of soldering wire to the relevant spot on the map, bend it to conform to the twists and turns of the trail, straighten the wire out, and place it along the scale of miles in the map legend.

This measurement method later proved to be surprisingly accurate and in any event was fairly sophisticated given the technological constraints at the time. Now, of course, everyone can use Google Maps, Garmins, and Fitbit devices to track workouts. These kinds of devices aren't the only new developments in the running world.

While the sport does not require these kinds of high-tech devices or any fancy equipment, and it's not mandatory to use or even know about the latest development in running shoes, there are certainly more bells and whistles available than there used to be. For younger kids, it's important to run more by feel and simply build a good aerobic base rather than focus on timed training sessions. For older athletes, having an edge—from lighter shoes to watches that record and monitor nearly everything—can't hurt. In general, athletes have access to better footwear and a number of different tools to enhance recovery and improve the quality of their training, and even a recreational jogger can benefit from better equipment.

FOOTWEAR

The biggest improvements in running equipment in recent decades have probably been in the area of shoe design. (Women may argue that true athletic bras have been a bigger blessing than anything else.) Long gone are the days when runners had to wear stiff, hard-leather contraptions to run in everything from sprints to marathons.

Appropriate running shoes are the most necessary piece of equipment for young athletes. To reduce any risk of injuries, it is important that athletes wear shoes that are consistent with their specific foot-strike patterns and overall biomechanics. Most running specialty stores have employees who can perform a quick assessment and make a recommendation of a brand and model. Athletes who have experienced recurring injuries may also benefit from seeing a specialist to get custom inserts that may help correct a specific and properly identified biomechanical issue.

Runners who find themselves dealing with chronic or recurring injuries may benefit from a gait analysis. This service is becoming increasingly available at running stores. It involves a specialist who watches a person run—sometimes, runners are even filmed running on an in-house treadmill—and determines not only what kinds of shoes or inserts he or she should wear but also any areas in the runner's body that may need to be strengthened.

Stability is key here. The more stable the foot is, the less excessive movement overall in terms of pushing or pulling on muscles, tendons, and joints throughout the lower body.

Brad stresses the importance of proper running shoes, particularly for young runners. When training with a club or school team, youth athletes may not have access to a lot of soft trails on which to run. If kids do the bulk of their training on hard surfaces, they should stay on top of replacing their running shoes on a regular schedule and not wait until the shoes have lost their support and cushioning.

Greg Weich, a high-school coach and running-store manager, notes that running-shoe technology has changed drastically since the 1980s and 1990s. Owing chiefly to better midsoles, training shoes are not only more comfortable and more responsive, but also tend to be more durable and longer-lasting. Certain models are made with unprecedented levels of cushioning and can even aid in recovery. Many of the shoes that have cropped up in the past half-dozen or so years, for example, have extra cushioning that simulate running on softer surfaces, even when the athlete is traipsing along asphalt.

While it is certainly not necessary for new runners, many young athletes wear spikes or racing flats when competing. These shoes are extremely light in weight with better traction, designed to help athletes move more efficiently when running faster. When deciding what kind of spikes to purchase, a young athlete must first know in which events she will be participating. Not all spikes are created equal. Some are made for sprinters, while others are made for long-distance track races and cross-country running, and each is designed to serve a certain purpose. Greg says that spikes for sprinters are engineered to get the runner up on his or her toes, while spikes for cross-country and distance running on the track have a more substantial and cushioned heel. The sprinter's spike will also have more actual spikes in the shoe's spike plate for maximum traction.

If a runner needs more support and stability while running, it's not worth risking injury racing in a much lighter, less supportive, and possibly more expensive spike or racing flat. Make sure to know the difference between all the different types of shoes before making a selection, and always ask a knowledgeable salesperson for help in making the right choice. (Again, think running specialty stores.) Above all, athletes should race in shoes they are familiar with and have had a chance to break in, not brand-new shoes out of the box.

TRAINING TECHNOLOGY

Running watches have come a long way in the past few decades. In the past, runners used watches with a simple timer function or even ditched the watch completely and ran by feel. Now, there are a number of global positioning satellite (GPS) watches available, and they are becoming more common, even among young athletes. There is a lot of value in being able to track time, distance, and pace; however, it is also important to stress to young athletes that they should not get too wrapped up in their pace on everyday runs. It can be detrimental to rely on a watch rather than the body to determine the pace of the day's workout, particularly on recovery runs, and getting too caught up in timing activities can detract from enjoying the moment and connecting to nature or the self.

That said, this type of technology can serve valuable purposes. Many of the more high-tech watch options also have a heart-rate monitor (HRM) feature. While most youth coaches don't think that heart-rate data is necessary on an everyday basis, this feature can provide valuable feedback. By using a heart-rate monitor, athletes can discover the correlation between effort and heart rate. Naturally, running at a faster pace will cause an athlete's heart rate to increase, but running up hills or against the wind will produce a similar effect.

Young and old athletes alike can be competitive, so using a heart-rate monitor to keep the pace reasonable during easy and recovery runs is helpful. Though there are numerous specific heart-rate "zones" for training, some coaches prefer using a simplified program that breaks the zones down into four main paces:

- interval and race pace or anaerobic capacity;
- long-distance race pace or threshold training;
- tempo pace or aerobic threshold;
- easy or active recovery.

Knowing a specific pace that correlates to certain efforts based on heart rate can help athletes make sure they are doing what is best for them rather than doing what another athlete is doing and training either too hard or not hard enough. Every person is built differently, possessing different strengths and weaknesses, and knowing the heart-rate range associated with each pace or effort is a good way to know where an athlete falls on the spectrum.

Online training logs are becoming very popular. Among the most common as of this writing are Strava, Training Peaks, Final Surge, and Garmin Connect. Several of these websites allow runners to upload training runs directly from their GPS watch. These online forums are great tools for tracking and saving training details. As a coach, it is very convenient to be able to look at each of your athletes' training logs, where they can record their mileage, workout results, and subjective impressions. Keeping up with training has become much easier since the days when everyone wrote things down by hand in a notebook.

Running logs are used primarily to see what kind of training works well and what kind of conditioning might be better left off the schedule in the future, but logs also help with organizing and setting goals. Without becoming overly fixated on continually bettering each workout or being too self-critical in general, runners can focus on key activities, exercises, and specific workouts to track. Noting the weather, fatigue levels, physical wellness, and mental motivation can also be helpful. With online logs, which allow runners to share data with friends and peers, people often hold themselves more accountable because they know others can see what they are doing. As a result, posting daily training sessions can be a great motivational tool.

RECOVERY TOOLS

Young athletes tend to be more durable and recover more quickly than older athletes. While those in the latter group typically spend more time and money on massage treatment and physical therapy, the youth crowd can still benefit from the consistent use of recovery tools. There are a number of different devices available that are not only effective and affordable, but also mobile and transportable. Some of the more commonly used recovery tools are The Stick, foam rollers, and Roll Recovery R8. The more economical athlete can achieve a great deal just from rolling out on a lacrosse or golf ball. If you go to a local middle- or high-school meet, you are likely to see runners adorned in brightly colored knee-length compression socks designed to massage sore calves and thus enhance recovery. Be sure to start gently with any recovery activities. Digging too hard into an already sore area can cause a damaging degree of inflammation and aggravate an injury rather than help it heal. Used correctly, however, recovery tools can be highly beneficial.

Nutrition bars and drinks are also essential for quick recovery after a race or hard workout. A number of different brands make quality products in various forms. Athletes can choose from protein bars, performance gels, and nutrition shakes. Bars and shakes with at least some protein should be used post-race or -workout because protein can help speed up the repair and recovery of muscles and can also reduce the release of the stress hormone cortisol. Gels and energy bars can be used before and during longer races. All of these products are easy to bring along to the track or cross-country course and can play a big role in refueling and rehydrating after a hard effort. The main thing to focus on, however, is getting plenty of liquids to prevent dehydration, especially in the heat.

Taking water on long runs is easier now than it was in the past. Specially designed hand-held water bottles and water bladders that are worn like backpacks are easy to use. Running in the heat can pose other problems like chafing and sunburn. Breathable lightweight hats, sunglasses, body glide, and sunscreen are available to protect a runner's skin and eyes. If running in the heat is a must, be sure to seek out as much shade as possible and take fluid breaks frequently, drinking as much as eight to twelve ounces every twenty minutes to offset sweat losses.

WINTER GEAR

If you live in an area with cold winters and heavy snowfall, then you know how uncomfortable it can be to get out for a run without the proper gear. Jackets, gloves, tights, and hats have become more lightweight and more comfortable. Today's options often incorporate vents to allow for breathability, and Gore-Tex ensures a waterproof exterior. Colder temperatures mean tighter muscles, and this not only makes it more difficult to run fast but can also increase the risk of injury. Having the proper running gear helps keep muscles warm and safe from being pulled or strained.

In cold conditions, it's best to wear layers. The proper winter wardrobe should include a pair of wind pants, a shell or outer jacket, several long-sleeved technical or "wicking" shirts, a vest, light running tights, insulated running pants, arm warmers, ear warmers, a hat, warm socks, gloves, a balaclava, and a face mask for when it gets very cold. Of course, it takes some experimenting to find what combination of clothing works to keep each runner comfortable. Some athletes love the cold and can tolerate exercising in clothing others would wear only when spring hits and the sun is out. It's better to start off wearing extra layers that can be shed along the way. Some runners will even wear a light backpack, so they can take out or store extra items.

Running on snow and ice obviously entails a high risk of taking a spill. There are a number of different traction tools available that can be easily slipped over your running shoes. YakTrax, a coiled contraption invented by an adventure athlete who saw a Sherpa mountain guide wearing an anti-slipping device while hiking in Nepal, is one of the most common brands. Some athletes even insert screws into the bottoms of their shoes for a homemade option.

SAFETY: RUNNING AT NIGHT

Whatever time of day an athlete chooses to run, safety should always be a consideration. Young runners should be encouraged to tell at least one person where they are going and when they expect to be back. If possible, coaches should advise their athletes to run with a partner or in a group. When the only option is to work out in the quiet morning before the sun is up or at night after it has gone down, runners of all ages should note some other useful safety tips.

1. Wear reflective clothing and avoid wearing dark colors.
2. Carry or wear a running ID.
3. Use a small hand-held flashlight or wear a running headlamp.
4. Bring a cell phone.
5. Choose routes that are well lit or generally well populated and familiar.
6. Be on the alert and be cautious.
7. Don't obliterate your hearing with music.

Some runners will carry a whistle or pepper spray if they go out alone. This is a good idea for both males and females who are in areas where there is wildlife that might act spontaneously and aggressively when craving a two-legged snack.

WOMEN'S RUNNING ATTIRE

Young girls who run might need different attire than their male counterparts. Most obvious is that young women usually need the support of a sports bra, which can also reduce chafing on the nipples. Some girls will need a more supportive bra while others might be fine with one that's not as structured. Women's running shoes are actually designed differently than men's because women's feet are typically different. Shoes for women are generally wider in the toebox area and narrower in the heel, whereas men's shoes are often more uniform. Both provide structure and support, but seek out shoes that fit your feet well.

While it's not necessary to spend a lot on fashion, and most schools and clubs provide uniforms for racing, it can be fun to incorporate some panache into your running wardrobe. Showing off your flair for style can give your confidence a boost. When you like what you wear, you tend to feel better, and what you wear doesn't necessarily have to be visible to the world, as the lady who paints smiley faces on her toenails the night before running a marathon will tell you. When she's feeling tired during the race, she can think about her toenails smiling up at her, and that eases some of the discomfort she experiences during the later miles of the event.

Women have a lot more to choose from than men when it comes to clothing. Today's market includes tutus that may represent a certain cause such as cancer research, running skirts, and brightly colored tops, shorts, and tights. Women tend to have wider hips, so women's shorts will be cut differently, and women's tops will often be smaller than men's. You want your shorts or running pants to stay comfortably in place without binding, and singlets, tops, and vests shouldn't be flapping around in the wind. Just as with shoes, you should give the clothing you buy a try before showing it off in a race.

④

RUNNING IN THE FAMILY

Mantra: *I create my own story*

Regardless of age, behind every great athlete, you will most likely find a committed, reliable support system. It has been said that it takes a whole village to raise a child, but this applies to athletes as well, especially young ones.

Support starts at home. Running is a sport that often literally runs in the family, and it's difficult to imagine any young person succeeding in something as challenging as competitive running without a solid level of family support. Such support can take various forms, from basic encouragement and positive feedback from mother, father, and siblings to parents who regularly run with their children, attend their competitions, and, in many cases, plan and oversee their training. You probably wouldn't be reading this book if you didn't have a child or close younger relative who runs, or if you didn't have parents who wish to be an active part of your own training.

Brad notes that not all kids are physically or emotionally capable of running long distances. Training for and racing long distances is not the same as doing a onetime event, and onetime or once-a-year events can be an enjoyable way for families to connect while exercising. Consistent long runs and frequent runs during the week probably aren't good for most younger athletes, though Brad was one of the rare exceptions who could handle high mileage. Still, kids shouldn't be prohibited from running if they like it, and parents can accompany kids in some of their workouts or at least cheer them on from the sidelines. Most people can find camaraderie in running with a team or with a coach, but the bonds of parents and siblings will almost always be deeper. Brad suggests that parents refrain from discouraging competition between siblings or teammates, but he also insists that they shouldn't push their kids unreasonably hard.

Almost nobody wants to be the stereotypical, overbearing "Little League" parent, and accordingly, encouragement doesn't have to take on an obnoxious air. As a parent, be willing to separate your hopes and dreams from those of your child, and never reward or punish your child because of how he or she performs in races. When you're enthusiastic, whether you're a parent, mentor, brother, or sister, determining restraint in this area might take some discipline, but listening to your children is just as important as cheering them on. Make sure your athlete knows that you're not going to take credit for his or her hard work. Allow the spotlight to shine where it's supposed to. The young runner's family role is one of support, not dictatorship or judgment.

FEEDBACK AND COMMUNICATION

For young athletes to be successful, they must believe that they have an open line of communication with both their parents and their coaches. If a youth runner doesn't feel as if he can talk openly about how he is feeling physically and psychologically, burnout and injury are more likely to occur, and some sort of breakdown is virtually inevitable. There must be direct and effective communication between coach and athlete, coach and parent, and parent and athlete. In order for a runner to be successful at the highest levels, this triangular relationship needs to be monitored, maintained, and strengthened over the years. This takes a tremendous amount of trust and openness from everyone involved.

A lack of honest and frank communication is unquestionably one of the biggest contributors to burnout in young athletes. When there isn't a consistent dialogue among the athlete, coach, and parent, it creates an environment in which the athlete feels he or she has very little control. Stress and pressure begin to build, and eventually the athlete becomes emotionally and mentally spent. Coaches and parents should encourage the athlete to be involved in the conversation rather than relegate her to the status of a bystander in her own athletic career. Allowing younger runners to look at training and competing as a choice rather than a mandate can set them up to enjoy the sport for a lifetime.

Asking for feedback from athletes is absolutely essential. As a coach or involved parent, you need to know how they are feeling emotionally, mentally, and physically. Young athletes don't always feel as if they can broach these topics on their own, and they sometimes have difficulty knowing how to explain what they are feeling. By asking questions, you can set the conversation in motion. While this feedback is an integral part of the athlete-coach relationship, you must also strive to make this feedback constructive and positive so as to not create a negative or punitive atmosphere.

Rebecca Walker, a runner and mother living in Westminster, Colorado, tries to give her strong-willed, independent, and very ambitious daughter, Ariel, sensible guidelines when it comes to running, but Ariel isn't bound by a specific training plan. The ten-year-old girl has a good sense of what works for her and what she wants to do when it comes to running. Without any real structure, Ariel has already come close to Rebecca's 26:58 personal best in the 5K by running a 28:12. Ariel runs when she feels like it and doesn't when she's not feeling up to it, which is ideal for a highly motivated child and is what her mother prefers. Rebecca doesn't force Ariel to run but supports her when she chooses to. The mother-daughter team usually goes out for a two- or three-mile run twice a week, and they make sure to incorporate fun into both their training runs and their racing endeavors.

It might shock some people that Ariel completed a 50K (31.1-mile) ultramarathon over two days, but she did it in a sensible way and with the guidance of her mother. It's important to recognize that some young children are wise beyond their years and have a good sense of what they need, while others need far more guidance. As a parent, you have to determine what seems rational versus what might end up harming your child. It can be difficult to establish the boundary between what's too much and what's not enough exercise, but the feedback your child gives you can help you define it. No matter what age a runner is, a parent or coach needs to be able to listen to what he or she says and ask the right questions that will help the athlete or young participant feel secure and comfortable on the path he or she has chosen.

Health maintenance, even in the absence of problems, is also critical. Always check in with your child's physician on at least a yearly basis to make sure your child is and continues to be healthy enough to run, and when the drive is there, allow her activity to flourish in the healthiest way possible.

SUPPORT

Whether you are a parent, other family member, or coach, there are many ways to support a young athlete. Some parents encourage their children to be active by going for runs with them. This method of getting involved—actually participating with them—shows that you care about their success and are willing to give your own time and energy to help them. It can also be a way to share the experience of running with each other, giving more depth to your relationship to your child in the context of the sport as well as generally.

When supporting young athletes, especially runners, there are a few things for parents to keep in mind. Focus on encouragement and keep up with what the athletes are learning through their sport rather than simply what their performance results are. At root level, effort is really the only aspect of the sport over which athletes have any control. As a parent or coach, communicate that all you are asking for is their best effort and not specific outcomes. Matching expectations with encouragement is the best way to create an environment in which young athletes can thrive. Keeping in line with this method, parents and coaches can emphasize both (what are seen as) important and unimportant competitions. By placing equal importance on each of the races and de-emphasizing stringent expectations, young athletes can learn to be more relaxed going into a race and will learn that the goal is to always put in their best effort when they toe the line, regardless of the context or what is riding on the outcome. When the athlete is older and more experienced, it's acceptable to put more energy into and peak for specific races.

Anyone who participates in the career of an athlete at a young age is not only a coach, parent, or mentor, but also a role model. This should be kept in mind at all times. Everything that you say or do is being observed and mentally indexed by your children, and if you coach, this is true of your athletes. Demonstrate the behaviors and attitudes that you want them to see and emulate. Assuming the role of a coach and leading by example is one of the most effective ways you can impact a young athlete. You will also create a sense of loyalty as it becomes evident to your athletes that you are willing to put in the same effort you are asking of them for years to come.

For eleven-year-old Lucy Alexander, watching her dad, Craig, a five-time world champion in the Ironman triathlon, was inspiring, but she grew up knowing she wanted to be her own person, separate from her father yet hardworking just like him. Whether she continues in athletics or changes her mind as she gets older, she knows that following her dreams, whatever they may be, takes discipline, dedication, and hard work.

Although leading by example is one of the best ways to instill good habits, one need not be an athlete to inspire young runners. Many outstanding coaches no longer run or have never run competitively, but they are adamant about and effective at helping others achieve their goals in life.

KEEP IT FUN

When running serves a way for your family to spend time together, it becomes even more important to keep it fun. That doesn't mean that every step of every run or workout will necessarily *feel* fun. If, however, the running environment is always accompanied by stress and pressure, both performance and relationship quality will be negatively affected. Sharing the sport of running with young athletes as a parent or coach is a great way to pass along something that they have the potential to enjoy for a lifetime and to then themselves pass along to the next generation. With that opportunity comes the risk of letting the competitive side of the sport exceed healthy limits and affect the health of the relationship outside of running.

Allow your athletes to have the opportunity to provide input about their training. Most of the time, you will find that they are willing and eager to put in the hard work, but by giving them some say in their training and racing, you will start to notice and recognize cues about how much fun they are having. Rebecca Walker left the race strategy up to her daughter for the ultramarathon she ran, but she did establish a few rules of her own and made sure that Ariel was getting enough food, water, and rest during the race. Ariel was excited and wanted to participate. She loved the encouragement she got along the race course from officials and other participants. This is the kind of experience that will keep a child eager to run and happy to come back the following year.

When you sense that kids are feeling uninspired or unmotivated, do something to bring the fun back and reignite the fire. Again, having fun and working hard are not mutually exclusive. You can incorporate a game into practice or offer a reward after a tough workout or competition to inject some life into training. A family can enjoy scavenger hunts, tag, fox-and-hounds, and other running games, and it doesn't have to cost anything to participate. Something to keep in mind is that taking a short break from running can also bring back the drive to participate.

Bean Wrenn, a competitive masters (over-forty) runner and mother of two, is careful about letting her children run what she considers too much. In her opinion, a half-marathon race or anything longer is too much for a youngster, unless the event is done in a purely fun and social way. Regarding racing a half-marathon, she says that she can't help but think that this kind of training must have some kind of negative impact on a child's growth. As a parent, she would not allow her children to run that far at such a young age. She doesn't think she herself ran that distance until she was about twenty years old. Bean tries to remind her kids to run because they enjoy it, not to seek her approval by doing it. She adds that it has to be something they want to do, not something she wants them to do.

When Bean let her daughter, Marist, run her first 10K at age seven, she ran with her and kept checking in with her daughter to see if Marist wanted to take walking breaks. The emphasis was on fun, and Marist loved it. She ran with her parents and only walked a few times. When the family members crossed the finish line, the young girl knew she wanted to do it again the following year.

In contrast to her daughter's strong drive to do well in races and get to the finish line as fast as she can, Bean's son, Gavin, is all about the experience of running. He will stop to enjoy the activities and entertainment along the side of the roads that include a slip-n-slide and food stops. Both kids end up with big smiles at the end of their races, evidence that they are each enjoying their experiences. Bean will keep allowing them to race, but she is careful about how much they train on a daily basis. In general, she prefers that they participate in other sports such as soccer and run only occasionally.

RUNNING GAMES FOR KIDS

Tag

Tag is played in a large area, usually outdoors. The boundaries of the area can be as small as a yard or as large as half a football field. One version of the game called "Sharks and Minnows" is best played in an area such as the latter. The game starts with one designated child acting as the shark. The rest of the children line up on one end of the designated area, and when the shark yells, "Go," they try to run across to the other side of the area, where they are then in a safety zone. If the shark tags anyone, that minnow turns into a shark and can chase the others. The game continues with the minnows going from one safety zone to another each time the sharks yell "go" until there is only one minnow left. At the end of the game, the one child left becomes the shark in the next game.

Water Relay

There are several versions of a water relay. Divide the children into as many teams as needed, so that there are at least three or four kids in each team. Fill one bucket of water for each team and place the buckets at the start line for each team and an empty bucket about 100 meters away directly across from the filled buckets. Give each child one plastic glass or cup and have them stand on the start line, one behind the other in each team. On "Go," the first child in each line will scoop up a glass of water and run as fast as he or she can to the empty bucket directly across. The child will then empty the glass into the bucket and run back to tag the next team member, and the game continues. The first team to fill the container with water is the winner.

Scavenger Hunt

Before the kids arrive, hide clues written on slips of paper within a designated area. Write six different clues for each team, but don't use any of the same clues for both. For example, if team A's first clue reveals a tree that the kids must run to, team B's first clue could reveal a bench instead. Whichever team finds all the clues first is the winner.

Red Light, Green Light

In this game, one child or mentor will be the stoplight at one end of a designated area, while the others will start at the opposite end and eventually try to be the first to cross the line where the stoplight is. To start, all the children form a line about fifty meters away from the stoplight. The stoplight faces the kids and says, "Green light." The kids are allowed to move toward the stoplight, but when the stoplight yells, "Red light," the kids must stop. Anyone who doesn't stop is sent back to the start line. The game continues until the first child crosses the line where the stoplight is. At this point, the one who is the winner can become the new stoplight.

Last Man Up Run

This is a fartlek style of running in which a team runs comfortably in a single-file line around a track or field. The game starts when the last person in line runs fast up to the front of the line to take over the lead place. When that person gets there, the next person at the end of the line runs up to the front of the line until everyone has had a chance to lead the pack.

Butterfly Game

For the butterfly game, kids will be running fast down a straightaway that will represent the body of the butterfly. It's best to do this exercise on a soft surface, so go to the park or find a field or playground where you can mark off a large area suitable for running. Set up cones or easily visible markers in the shape of a butterfly. Make sure the shape of the butterfly is symmetrical on each side (the wings), with a straight line down the center (the body). Start the kids off jogging in a single-file line around one side of the wings. When each one gets to the top of the body, he or she will sprint down the center. Once the child has reached the end of the body, he or she walks around the other wing. Make sure no two kids are sprinting at the same time.

Capture the Flag

Find a large area to set the boundaries. Ideally, the space should be a rectangle or square. Divide the area directly down the middle to form two equal "territories," one for each team. Form two teams, and give each a flag or something that represents a flag like a brightly colored T-shirt. Also, mark off a small area on the side of each territory that will serve as the jail for each team.

Have each group strategically place their flag somewhere in their territory. The flag must be at least partially visible and not impossible to retrieve. Once a team places their flag in its position, they cannot move it.

The goal of the game is to go into the opposing team's territory and then find and capture the other team's flag. Then the child must bring it back safely without being tagged. If a player is tagged by someone from the other team, he must go to their prison until one of his own team members can come rescue him by tagging him, at which point they can both travel safely back to their own territory. The game ends when one team successfully brings the flag of the opposing team into their own territory.

Pop the Balloon Relay

Set the boundaries for the relay by marking two parallel lines about twenty-five feet apart from each other. Divide the kids into two teams, and have the kids form two lines next to each other, both on the start line. Place a big pile of balloons on the other line facing the kids. On the start, the first two kids from each team must race to the pile of balloons, grab one, and try to pop it as quickly as possible. The kids can sit on the balloon, step on it, or figure out another way to pop it without using any pins or other objects. Once the child pops the balloon, she runs back to the start line to tag the next team member in line. The game continues like this until everyone has had a chance to pop a balloon. The team with the members who pop all their balloons first is the winner.

Obstacle Course

One doesn't need an official U.S. Navy SEALs obstacle course to get a good workout. In fact, anyone can create an obstacle course in a park or backyard. Obstacle courses can vary in distance and in the number of obstacles included. The course can include running up and down hills, jumping over pool noodles on the ground, racing around orange cones, climbing up and down the monkey bars, running through sand, carrying weights, or hula hooping at different stations.

Beanbag Race

Find a large flat area outside or inside in a gym. Mark two lines opposite each other about fifteen feet apart on the ground. Give each participant a beanbag and have the players stand on the starting line lined up next to each other and facing the line on the opposite side. The contestants have to get to the opposite side in one of the following ways: crawling, while balancing a beanbag on his back, running, while squeezing a beanbag between her knees, or doing a crab walk while balancing the beanbag on her stomach. Start the game with a "Ready, set, go!" and let the players race toward the finish line. A participant has to start over if his beanbag falls before he reaches the finish line.

CREATE BOUNDARIES

When you become involved with your child's athletics, you need to both create and respect boundaries. Know when and where to talk about running and when to leave the subject behind. One of the most rewarding activities for parents everywhere is watching their children compete in a sport they love. Unfortunately, in an informal survey that lasted three decades, Bruce E. Brown and Rob Miller of Proactive Coaching, LLC went out on their own and polled hundreds of college athletes who admitted what their worst memory of their sport was. By far, the most popular response was riding home from a competition with their parents. While this may be alarming and even serve as a discouragement to become heavily involved in your child's athletics, it shouldn't. The result simply illustrates the influence you have when it comes to your kids and sports.

Before your child begins entering races, find out what makes him or her tick. Some kids prefer to be calm and aloof before events, while others thrive on being talkative and animated. Both are acceptable ways to deal with stress. After races, some crave attention, while others like to have some time to themselves. Immediately after a race or important workout, briefly check in with your child or athlete to see what he or she needs. Later, you can discuss the events with your athlete in more detail and think about both things that were done right and things that could have been done better. Once this evaluation has taken place, let it go and move forward and encourage your athlete to do the same. Discouraging your athlete from brooding over unsatisfactory performances is crucial. Nearly thirty years after his high-school running career ended, Kevin, who had a habit of threatening to throw out all of his running shoes after subpar races, remains grateful to his mother for always saying the right things to keep competitive running in perspective.

Be sure that you discuss topics related to athletics at the appropriate time and place. It's necessary to recognize where these types of conversations should occur. Respect the times and events that are seen as family time (e.g., family dinners) and don't bring specific details about your child's sport into these spaces.

Another boundary to be aware and respectful of is the one that exists between parent and coach. If you are a parent heavily involved in your child's running but you aren't his or her coach, respect the coach's role and let him do his job. Any coach involved in youth athletics is aware of the importance of parent involvement. Most often, they encourage and welcome parents who are also supportive and invested in their child's athletic results. However, parents that overstep their boundaries and attempt to influence the coach too much will end up disrupting the synergy that is required in any team situation. Don't give advice to your child that contradicts the information the coach provides. On the other side of the coin, coaches must recognize when they are overstepping a boundary and taking on a parent's role. On the whole, communication between coaches and parents is as vital as child-parent and coach-athlete communication.

NUTRITION FOR HEALTH AND PERFORMANCE

Mantra: *I love and accept myself*

Just eat it. —Weird Al Yankovic, 1985

Even the most complicated areas of scientific study enjoy a general trend toward clearer facts and declining uncertainty. Biologists describe new, exotic species of plants and animals; astronomers discover more and more planets orbiting distant stars; medical researchers develop promising new medications and unlock the genetic secrets underlying crippling diseases.

Nutrition, on the other hand, seems to only pile on more questions every year without satisfactorily answering long-standing ones. Whether you're athletic or sedentary, young or old, a health professional or a health-care consumer, you're continually forced to maneuver a minefield of contradictory advice and abrupt shifts in expert consensus. Are fats the enemy or not, and if so, what kind? Carbs are a must—but wait, they're also evil. Is organic food demonstrably more healthful, or is it simply money wasted on feeding your sense of superiority rather than your organs and tissues? And what's the real deal with gluten, trans fats, high-fructose corn syrup (HFCS), and GMOs? Given this tumultuous landscape, it's little wonder that eating disorders among younger people remain rampant even as obesity rates in the same age cohort continued to rise throughout the early twenty-first century.

THE EVOLUTION OF NUTRITIONAL ADVICE

When Kevin and Brad were running as teens in the 1980s, they were told very few specific things about how to nourish their developing, athletic selves. Broad, unfocused advice ruled the day: "Don't eat too much junk food (whatever that is)," "Eat your veggies," "Make sure you take in lots of carbohydrates," and that old nugget of grand insight, "Drink plenty of fluids." Notions of carb-protein-fat ratios and avoiding specific additives such as HFCS were years into the future, and—while Gatorade was a staple for many—the multibillion-dollar sports-drink industry of today did not exist. Discussions of veganism and vegetarianism were rare and regarded as the purview of hippies, if not outright cranks—certainly nothing suitable for athletes. The idea of stuffing vitamins and minerals into something essentially resembling a candy bar was nowhere in evidence.

But that era of simplicity has passed, and this doesn't have to be a bad thing. In a sporting world of limitless supplements, too many powders and energy bars and beverages to count, and a barrage of conflicting advice from online sources, the mainstream media, and even medical professionals, it's critical for young runners, their parents, and their mentors to keep the fundamentals of sports nutrition in mind, for these haven't changed over the years and—at least in theory—never will.

THE BASIC MORSELS

Only the essentials of general human nutrition are given in this chapter; for those with a special interest in the relevant science, there are, of course, entire books, websites, and other media devoted to a thorough and well-researched treatment of this compelling and controversial subject. For present purposes, what's here should suffice.

Foods consist of three so-called *macronutrients*—carbohydrates and proteins, each of which supply four calories per gram, and fats, which provide nine calories per gram. For reference, most people burn about eighty to one hundred calories per mile of running. Carbohydrates, long considered the endurance athlete's chief dietary ally, are found in a wide variety of foods, from sweets such as candy to staples like rice and potatoes. Sugars such as sucrose (table sugar) and fructose (fruit sugar) are "simple" carbohydrates, while starches like breads and pasta are complex carbohydrates; the latter get their name from the fact that the body takes longer to break them down into energy. Proteins are found chiefly in foods of animal origin—meats and dairy products, for example. Protein is not much of a direct energy source but instead is critical for rebuilding muscle tissue broken down during training. Fats are, again, found mainly in foods associated with hooves, fins, and wings—olives and avocados are notable exceptions—and provide the bulk of the energy athletes need for lower-intensity endurance exercises such as walking or slow running. Medical types typically advise folks of all ages, whether active or sedentary, to limit their consumption of fats, in particular saturated and "trans" fats, as these may be associated with a high risk of developing cardiovascular disease (the extent to which this is true remains ever-controversial and seems to relate more to individual people's handling of fats than anything else). Cholesterol, another traditional marker for heart-disease risk, is found in most animal fats.

In addition to these macronutrients, your body requires a range of vitamins and minerals—at least thirty of them. Physiologic "doses" of these are measured not in grams but in much smaller amounts—milligrams (in the case of most minerals) and micrograms (most vitamins). Vitamins—organic compounds that are much less stable than minerals, which maintain their structure under a variety of conditions—are best known by their letters: A, various types of B, C, D, E, K, to name the most common. Minerals, on the other hand, including iron, calcium, and magnesium, come right off the periodic table of the elements familiar to any chemistry student. Both types of compounds participate in functions ranging from nerve-signal transmission to bone strengthening to red-blood-cell formation. In short, they may be small in mass, but they do big jobs.

Vitamins A, C, and E are the *antioxidants*—they help stave off damage to your cells resulting from the formation of compounds called free radicals during normal metabolic reactions. These are found in fruits and vegetables—the more colorful, the richer in antioxidants a particular veggie tends to be. The B vitamins—chief among them thiamine, riboflavin, niacin, and B12—are involved in the release and transfer of biochemical energy as well as protein synthesis, the latter critical in growing athletes, since they are continually breaking down and rebuilding tissue at an unusually high rate.

Vitamins can also be subdivided on the basis of their chemical solubility. Vitamins A, D, E, and K are the *fat-soluble* vitamins; if people overdo it with any of them, any excess is stored in their fatty tissues and liver and occasionally can reach toxic levels. The B vitamins and vitamin C are water-soluble; they are absorbed easily into your bloodstream and circulate freely in the large fraction of your body—about two-thirds—consisting of water.

As with many things in medicine, the role of vitamins and minerals often becomes most evident in times of deficiency. Notably, in the endurance-sports world, insufficient iron intake thanks to inappropriate or rigid diets in the context of increased physical demands can lead to *anemia*. This is a distressingly common condition among endurance athletes and in particular young women runners, who frequently manifest "picky" dietary habits while losing iron each month in the blood loss in menses. Anemia is diagnosed using a blood test that measures hemoglobin levels, but a health provider can run a so-called anemia panel to look at levels of associated compounds such as serum ferritin. This helps reveal whether a young runner might be on her way to anemia before she actually gets there, which in turn serves to guide nutritional advice. Iron is found classically in red meats (heme iron—the most easily absorbed kind) along with fortified grains and leafy green vegetables such as spinach. Once anemia has been established, supplementation in pill or liquid form may be necessary to restore normal iron status. Athletes and coaches should be aware of this bane above all other mineral deficiencies, for over the course of a serious distance runner's career, the chances that she will become clinically iron-deficient are perhaps better than the chances that she won't.

Understand that throughout this chapter, Kevin and Brad do not intend to sell people on any special diet or declare any foods either musts or no-nos. There is simply too much variation in the way people handle given foods from person to person (Jack might be lactose-intolerant; Jill might love nothing more than cow's milk as a source of protein) for dogma to have any place in this discussion. Instead, as the rest of the chapter stresses, the aim is to get young runners, their parents, and their coaches on the same page when it comes to developing a *healthy relationship with food* and ensuring that runners regard nutrition not as a chore but indeed as a *pleasurable and informed daily indulgence*. People face enough challenges in this world without turning food into an adversary, too.

DISORDERED EATING AND YOUNGSTERS' RELATIONSHIP WITH FOOD

This book does not assume the task of going into detail about pop-culture standards of thinness and the media's frequently cited role in perpetuating unrealistic ideas about what it means to be attractive, fit, or thin. Kevin and Brad acknowledge that this is a real problem and that Western society is awash in troubling hypocrisy when it comes to women and eating disorders; many of the same publications that routinely publish articles about women with these afflictions feature images of ultra-skinny models who, even if they're not actively starving themselves, certainly don't appear to be remotely well nourished. But we believe that food, body image, and nutrition would be a battleground for lots of young runners even without the problems in this area affecting greater society and that athletes face unique issues in the realm of eating disorders.

Taking a step back for the moment, perhaps the most important lesson a young runner can learn not directly related to training or racing is how to read his or her body from day to day. A critical aspect of this is knowing how to properly fuel that body. Knowledge of sound nutrition alone isn't enough; it is absolutely crucial for athletes to develop a positive and healthy relationship with their physical selves and the foods they eat.

Running is a methodically demanding sport that eventually weeds out those who cannot maintain their health. Unfortunately, it's possible to thrive as a competitor for a while even while carrying on nutritional habits—self-starvation and binging and purging being the most common offenders—ranging from negligent to overtly self-destructive. History has shown beyond a doubt that runners who become too lean will eventually fall by the wayside. It may take mere months or it may take a few years, but it will happen, and these bad habits can lead to long-term consequences. Yet an equally inescapable reality is that runners who are too heavy court injury with every step and underperform in races. Because these competing factors sit on opposite sides of an important line, it's critical to have outside guidance in this area.

With the runners he advises, Brad elects not to focus on numbers on a scale or athletes' body-mass index, or BMI (your weight in kilograms divided by the square of your height in meters). Instead, he relies on feedback from his athletes about how they're feeling overall, their energy levels, and so on. He knows that weight can fluctuate a great deal even within a single day, especially during the heat of summer when an athlete's fluid levels can rise and fall markedly. So he looks at other factors to determine the health of his runners. Is the athlete consistently training and racing well while avoiding injuries, especially injuries of the sort—for example, recurrent stress fractures—that may suggest nutritional problems? Apart from psychological struggles, there really are only a few reasons other than misguided or inadequate training or insufficient rest that an athlete doesn't run well. If an athlete is feeling worn down despite getting enough sleep and following his or her personalized training schedule, Brad might suggest eating more. Athletes should be able to get through hard workouts along with the school day or work day without crashing or feeling excessively fatigued. It is important for the coach and athlete to maintain an honest and open dialogue. If an athlete is struggling with any issue with the potential to affect her running, including concerns with her weight or an outright eating disorder, she should feel comfortable approaching her coach.

Importantly, a coach doesn't have to be an expert in nutrition to help his or her athletes. He does, however, need to secure their trust. It's good practice to refer athletes who might need some extra guidance in the area of food intake to a dietician or nutritionist. In cases in which an individual is obviously struggling with her training because she isn't eating enough and is having difficulty with related matters such as body image, it may be helpful to suggest to her parents that they schedule a consultation with the family doctor, who may provide a referral to a sports psychologist.

It is critical that kids who are in the grip of an eating disorder—be it in the early stages or under the lash of a long-standing problem—not be ashamed about suffering from the disease. There's a long-standing paradox when it comes to eating disorders: almost all runners, including young people, know that these afflictions are common in certain sports and disciplines, treatable, and far from a sign of moral decay or a lack of mental fortitude. Yet when you're the one who actually has such a disorder, you think of yourself as weak, wrongheaded, and some sort of strange outlier.

Recognize, too, that not all types of disordered eating go by formal or familiar names. Anorexia athletica—an obsessive preoccupation with food, diet, and exercise—in distance runners, especially male distance runners, often goes undetected simply because so many very thin people populate the sport's higher levels. It may not be obvious that unusual thinness in some cases represents more than the result of hard training and genetic tendencies. In some cases, a significant degree of silent mental turmoil accompanies and drives being exceptionally lean. For the most part, those with anorexia athletica no longer truly enjoy their exercise, and both their training and racing represent the endpoints of cold psychological obligations to work out and perform up to par. Runners who are overly controlling with respect to diet or those with EDNOS—eating disorders not otherwise specified—generally don't experience lasting performance gains (and derive little real or lasting satisfaction from the gains they do make). Wasting too much mental energy on adhering to a specific set of rigid rules concerning food—e.g., weighing portions, sharply limiting grams of fat with every meal—can, in both the short term and in seasons and years to come, be detrimental to overall health and well-being.

Dealing with kids is not the same thing as dealing with adults, so a coach's role changes as an athlete develops. Coaching young runners requires more accountability and a greater investment. It's the coach's job to shepherd athletes to their next phase of running as physically healthy and in as sound a psychological condition as possible. Allowing a successful but clearly deteriorating athlete to continue training and racing without proper nourishment evidences a lack of accountability on the part of the coach. At some point, it's the coach's responsibility to intervene in some way if an athlete is unable to properly take care of his or her general health and nutrition.

VERY OFTEN, A LIFE-OR-DEATH ISSUE

In March of 2006, a twenty-year-old former standout runner and honor student from Wisconsin named Alexandra DeVinny died of cardiac arrest, one of the complications of anorexia nervosa that frequently leads to fatal outcomes. At the time of her death, Alex, who less than three years earlier had recorded a very fast 10:53 for 3,200 meters to win her high-school state championship in that event as a junior, weighed an astonishing seventy pounds at 5'8". In the last years of her life, her illness was no secret—by the middle of her senior year, her running career had already dissolved along with her plans to compete in college—and she had ample family and medical support, but the viciousness of her case ultimately claimed her. More to the point, she had begun showing the signs of an eating disorder when she was only nine years old—a scenario echoed with increasing and unsettling urgency across America. Alex's high-school coach admitted in a 2006 *New York Times* article that he was simply at a loss to confront what he thought he might be seeing as Alex's weight eroded into dangerous levels and in the wake of her death was so distressed that he quit coaching girls.

But did he learn something? This is where the oft-cited but just-as-often-dismissed lines of communication have to be open. When Kevin coached high-school girls, they were comfortable telling him when, for example, their menstrual periods had stopped or when they had any concerns about their weight. On the whole, he was fortunate to have an unusually strong and close relationship with the parents of the runners. But if you are a coach who needs to strive a little harder to create such a situation, it's absolutely essential that you do so. If you are serious about your role as a mentor and coach and not just trying to fill space before a better job or better coach comes along, you must accept that dealing with the overall well-being of your runners is not something you can simply neglect and that eating disorders are inextricably woven into the sport.

Lize Brittin, a two-time Foot Locker finalist and world-class mountain runner who nearly died of anorexia more than once in her twenties and is now years into recovery, writes in her memoir *Training on Empty* about the built-in tension between the need to limit excess weight and the perils of becoming too thin. She quotes world-renowned running and triathlon coach Bobby McGee:

> From a plain exercise physiological point of view, the lighter the runner, the higher their VO2 Max. This is their ability (measured in milliliters) to utilize oxygen per kilogram of body weight. This is a key performance factor in endurance events. The lighter the athlete, therefore, the better they perform—hence the warped "reward" that these athletes receive for losing so much weight. Of course this period of heightened performance is finite as the effects of the illness start to shut down the system with its all-too-often inevitable outcome—terrible, terrible illness, anguish and even death.

Lize emphasizes that the job of a coach is not an easy one. If runners provide their coaches with incomplete or misleading information—not just about nutrition but about things like how much training they've done over the summer and how fast, etc.—then those coaches cannot make sound decisions regarding individual training. After a while, an athlete with an established eating disorder is likely to bend the truth without even thinking about it. Lies about training volume, food intake, and actual weight are standard. As the author of the *Times* article relates, even the best-trained psychologist can have a difficult time filtering through the deceptive acts and statements that can accompany an eating disorder. So it's no surprise that, while many coaches are now encouraged to identify a physical consequence of training hard while undereating known as the *female athlete triad*—disordered eating, the cessation of menstrual periods, and osteoporosis—few of them, especially at the middle-school and high-school levels, are prepared to deal with the psychological aspects of an eating disorder and may not understand that addressing these aspects goes far beyond recognizing the triad and knowing the *general* or *typical* symptoms of an eating disorder. For example, a runner with bulimia—willfully excessive food consumption followed by "purging" either by throwing up, taking laxatives, engaging in long periods of exercise, or a combination of these—may not develop amenorrhea, and not all women or girls who are underweight lose their periods. So while it's important to know that an eating disorder can lead to amenorrhea and bone loss, it's also critical to realize that not every sufferer will show these symptoms. And clearly, the female triad doesn't appear in boys, who can also develop eating disorders and who have come forward about this in greater numbers as the twenty-first century has crawled beyond its infancy.

Also, while the focus here is on girls, young male runners with eating disorders are becoming identified more and more often. Boys and men have never been immune to anorexia and bulimia but historically have been able to fly more easily under the radar, not only because they are less likely to come forward but also because it's rare for anyone to suspect even a very scrawny male runner of having an eating disorder. Indeed, whereas the appearance of very thin girls often serves by itself as an alarm bell even in instances where no eating disorder is present, equally thin boys are more often a source of amusement to their peers. Kevin addressed the topic of males with eating disorders in a *Running Times* article, "The Thin Men." Be aware as a coach, parent, or teammate that while boys do fall victim to EDs far less frequently than girls do, male runners with EDs are far from a statistical rarity and can carry on untreated for years in a nearly impenetrable wall of shame because they feel like "freaks" or that they have relinquished their necessary masculinity. As always, be sensitive in your approach to these athletes.

The take-home messages here are that coaches must be willing to educate themselves about eating disorders, be forthright with their athletes and their athletes' parents about potential or existing eating issues, and know the limits of their ability to counsel athletes in these realms, so that they can encourage young runners to get outside help if necessary.

WARNING SIGNS OF AN EATING DISORDER

- Weight loss or gain, especially extreme or sudden
- Isolation or withdrawing from others
- Preoccupation with food, weight, or body image
- Fear of eating, eating certain foods, or eating around others
- Rigid routines, diets, and thinking
- Low self-esteem
- Eating large quantities of food quickly in one sitting or restricting
- Refusing to eat certain foods but cooking for others or talking about food excessively
- Hoarding food or hiding it
- Skin discoloration, puffiness, or dark circles under the eyes
- Wearing baggy clothing

STAYING TRUE TO YOURSELF

Everyone is, to some extent and usually a significant one, a product of the society in which he or she is raised—its norms, its taboos, and its expectations. Few people are as independent and detached as they like to think. Runners fancy themselves to be more free-thinking than most, but in truth, most of them strive mightily to resemble other runners—except that they want to be better. Distance runners see their leanest, hungriest-looking peers excelling and wish to outperform them, not only on the track but on the scale as well. This sets the stage perfectly for a great many young runners to develop eating disorders, and with millions of people routinely posting only their most flattering "selfies" on social media, the problem isn't going anywhere. But *no* eating disorder is obligatory. The more everyone involved in the training of an athlete is aware of the causes of an eating disorder, the more the athlete can avoid unhealthy behaviors. She doesn't have to be negatively affected by the unrealistic ideals many in the beauty industry—despite their ongoing protestations to the contrary—actively promote. She need not be a slave to peer pressure or change her behaviors or appearances as a result of what outsiders, many of them perhaps well-meaning but naive, might say. Her number-one focus should be on feeling strong and healthy, not on looking a certain way. Becoming ultra-thin and running well on the surface look like complementary goals. We wish to stress emphatically here that in the long term, successful careers in sports are never the result of rigorous calorie restriction. Some runners who engage in this wind up looking more wasted away than others, but in any case, chronic energy deprivation always leads to problems. This can be easily confirmed by any objective fact-hunter.

The bottom line is that runners have to be healthy to run well. "Healthy" doesn't just mean free of injuries and colds and other everyday, and sometimes unavoidable, offenders. Up to a certain point, and if someone starts off with real mass to lose, being at a lower weight can help her—no one is denying this. But distance running fundamentally requires *strength*, and a poorly fueled body will not only never perform to the best of its ability; it will usually fail in an ongoing and calamitous cascade of endocrine, musculoskeletal, and even psychiatric problems.

"DIETS" VERSUS NOURISHMENT

In the 1970s, the idea of a "crash diet"—nothing more than extreme caloric restriction or even fasting in an effort to quickly drop weight, with the composition of any food eaten more or less unimportant—was still alive and flourished in some circles. In the late 1980s, food makers, journalists, and a fair number of health professionals launched a full-frontal assault against fat—with nine calories a gram and the potential to clog your arteries beyond all recognition, it was deemed a non-starter, and in the endurance-sports world, this further energized an already powerful focus on consuming carbohydrates, especially complex carbs such as pasta, rice, and whole-grain breads. All the while, the weight of a typical American rose confoundingly higher every year, with the trend reaching into younger and younger age groups. By the late 1990s, with fat-free snacks and other foods generously dotting supermarket shelves and the pogrom against fat having proven useless from a public-health standpoint, carbohydrates, thanks chiefly to a book by Dr. Robert Atkins, became the new focus of demonization. A society that had just gotten used to being steadfastly against fats was suddenly convinced that going "low-carb" was a weight-loss panacea. This trend, repackaged from the "Atkins diet" to the "Keto diet"—more on this below—and still more than widespread as of 2014, swept up a surprising number of endurance athletes, even those who had relied on an intake consisting of at least 75 percent of calories from carbs to fuel themselves for many years, to great effect.

But the debate was only starting with the low-carb craze. Being a vegetarian (i.e., eating no meat) or a vegan (i.e., consuming nothing of animal origin, including eggs and dairy products) had never been unheard of in the athletic world, but as the twenty-first century entered its second decade, an increasing number of athletes began favoring such regimens, many of them driven at least in part by ethical concerns. Meanwhile, the spawn of these diets began showing up everywhere, each of them becoming hot buttons in the worlds of blogs and social media and giving rise to best-selling books with alacrity: people who became friendly with the "Paleo diet" were matched bite-for-bite by folks who staunchly advocated carbohydrate restriction to the point that the body was forced into a semi-starvation mode for short periods, a metabolic state that most physicians classify as hazardous. And just to confuse the issue further, a lot of people started urging others to dispense of things such as gluten, the presence of which in one's diet is detrimental only to those people with a specific inability to process and digest it properly.

The authors aren't experts on any of these "diets" and frankly don't care to be. What their experience has told them is that no athlete in serious training can neglect a well-known set of critical players in the nutrition game, no matter where they come from. In brief, these include:

- *Iron.* Many athletes in heavy training who consume a "normal" American diet—that is, one consisting of at least some red meat on a regular basis—are at risk for becoming anemic. It's no surprise, then, that those who eschew red meat altogether are at higher risk, particularly women. Runners should have their iron levels checked every year at their annual check-ups and in some cases, such as when there is a history of iron deficiency, more often than this. Some runners need to take a supplement such as ferrous sulfate to maintain or increase their iron and hemoglobin levels, and taking such supplements with vitamin C increases their absorption fourfold. Heme iron—the type found in meat—is absorbed with far greater efficiency than iron found in vegetables or grains.
- *Protein.* Estimates of how much protein athletes need to take to help replace muscle tissue broken down by training vary, but a good guideline is about 1.5 grams per kilogram of body weight, or about 0.7 grams per pound of body weight. A 140-pound person, therefore, should look to take in at least 100 grams of protein a day, with good sources being egg whites, lean meats, and skim milk—for non-vegans and non-vegetarians, of course. Athletes who forgo animal products usually turn to a combination of beans and grains, quinoa, nuts, tofu, and the like to make up the difference.
- *Vitamin B12.* This vitamin has iron's back: it is essential in the formation of new red blood cells, although unlike iron, it does not actually become a component of those cells. Iron can be stored for years in the liver. Critically, vitamin B12 is not found in any plant foods (unless they are fortified) and is therefore absent from the diets of vegans, but not necessarily vegetarians since it is found in eggs, milk, and other dairy products. Vegan athletes should therefore discuss a sensible, ongoing B12 supplementation plan with their health professionals to prevent a deficiency, which can cause a condition known as pernicious anemia and affect your strength and balance as well.

PUTTING IT TOGETHER:
EATING AROUND COMPETITION

You may have wandered into this chapter specifically to learn what to eat the night before or the morning of a race. If so, we're sorry to keep you in suspense! In brief, for shorter events—say, anything lasting an hour or less, which includes pretty much any race a younger runner is apt to tackle seriously—you don't have to do anything significant outside your everyday routine as long as that routine is sound. It might take some experimenting to find foods to eat before competition that sit well, but generally easily digestible items such as oatmeal, toast with peanut butter, energy bars, or yogurt with fruit provide fuel without upsetting your stomach. Do any experimenting in practice, not before a race.

During the first fifteen to twenty minutes after a big effort in a workout or race, be sure to eat a snack that contains the right mix of protein and carbohydrates, about six grams of protein to thirty grams of carbohydrates. This will help delay cortisol secretion and ultimately aid in the recovery process. A nourishing meal an hour or two after this will also help you feel better more quickly. Of course, drinking enough fluids with and in between meals is essential to prevent dehydration.

SAMPLE MEALS

Athletes need to make sure that they are getting adequate nutrition and enough calories in order to handle their training loads. Without proper nutrition, the body won't be able to perform at an optimal level, and the risk of injury will increase.

Pre-race: Night Before

- Pasta with tomato sauce, grated cheese, and a salad
- Turkey sandwich with lettuce, tomato, mustard, mayo, and a pickle
- Vegetable pizza
- Tofu stir fry with vegetables
- Stuffed potatoes
- Grilled salmon with brown rice and sautéed vegetables
- Chicken breast with spinach and quinoa salad
- Poached eggs on a bed of rice and vegetables with sautéed avocado
- Veggie burger with sweet potato fries
- Pita bread stuffed with falafel, hummus, lettuce, tomato, cucumber, and yogurt sauce

Pre-race: Hours Before

Focus more on carbohydrates with a 4:1 carbohydrate to protein ratio.

- Energy bar
- Banana and 1 Tbsp. peanut butter
- Seed bread toasted with tsp. butter and 1 Tbsp. jam

- Oatmeal or rice with berries and almond butter
- Yogurt with dried cereal
- Rice and one poached egg
- Bagel with cream cheese
- Toaster waffle with 1 Tbsp. syrup
- Sautéed sweet potato with 1 tsp. olive oil drizzled on top
- Blueberry muffin

Post-race Snack: Within an Hour of Finishing

Aim for a 3:1 carbohydrate to protein ratio.

- Recovery sports drink
- Berry smoothie with protein powder
- Protein bar
- Bagel or crackers and peanut butter
- Banana and yogurt
- Chocolate milk
- Granola cereal with yogurt and strawberries
- ½ chicken salad sandwich
- Breakfast burrito
- Silver dollar pancakes with almond butter

Post-race Meal after Racing or a Hard Workout

Aim for about twenty grams of protein.

- Grilled chicken, salad, baked sweet potato, and sautéed zucchini
- Lean hamburger with french fries and a spinach salad
- Oven-baked nachos with cheese, beans, salsa, chicken or tofu, and a salad
- Vegetable omelet with whole wheat toast
- Smoothie with 1 banana, frozen fruit, ½ avocado, 1 cup Greek yogurt, honey, and kale
- Vegetable soup with ½ a turkey sandwich
- Chili with crackers and crudités
- Sautéed salmon, rice, and cooked vegetables
- Black bean and quinoa salad with feta cheese and toast on the side
- Pork chop with cucumber and avocado salad
- Vegan option: BBQ tempeh sandwich on a whole wheat bun with lettuce, tomato, onion, mustard, and bean sprouts

PRE-RACE RECIPE: OVERNIGHT OATMEAL IN A JAR

¹/₃ cup rolled oats
1–2 Tbsp. almond butter
¹/₃ cup milk or almond milk

1 Tbsp. honey or maple syrup
Pinch each salt and cinnamon

In an 8-oz. jar, place all ingredients and stir well. The almond butter doesn't need to be completely blended into the mixture. Secure the lid on the jar and place it in the refrigerator overnight.

PRE-RACE DINNER RECIPE: STUFFED POTATOES (SERVES 4)

4 medium russet potatoes
1½ cup chopped broccoli
½ red bell pepper chopped
1 clove garlic
1 Tbsp. olive oil
1/4 cup chopped fresh chives

½ cup low-fat sour cream or Greek yogurt
1 cup shredded cheddar cheese
1 cup diced smoked turkey
Salt and pepper to taste
2 Tbsp. chopped fresh parsley

Wash, pierce with a sharp knife, and bake or microwave potatoes until soft. Set aside. Turn the oven to 375 degrees.

Sauté garlic about one minute until it begins to brown. Stir in broccoli and cook while stirring until it begins to soften, about two minutes. Add in the red pepper and cook about one or two more minutes.

Combine the cooked vegetables with the turkey, sour cream, ½ cup of the cheddar cheese, ¼ cup chives, salt, and pepper in a bowl. When the potatoes are cool, cut off the top one-fourth and carefully scoop out the inner flesh leaving the skins intact. Add the inner flesh to the filling mixture and gently mash together.

Place the potato shells onto a lightly greased baking dish and fill them with an equal amount of filling. Sprinkle the remaining cheese onto the tops, and bake the stuffed potatoes about 20 to 25 minutes or until the cheese on top has melted and the filling is hot.

Cool slightly before garnishing with chopped parsley and serving. Serve with a chopped green salad.

POST-RACE SNACK RECIPE:
SNACK BAR (MAKES 8 SERVINGS)

1 cup cashews	¼ cup shredded coconut
¾ cup pitted medjool dates	¼ tsp. salt
¾ cup dried figs	pinch of nutmeg
zest of ½ lemon	⅓ cup raw pumpkin seeds

Line an 8-inch baking pan with parchment paper or Saran wrap and set aside.

Pulse cashews in food processor until crumbly. Place processed nuts into a bowl and set aside.

Pulse dates and figs in the food processor until finely chopped. Add all other ingredients except the pumpkin seeds to the dried-fruit mixture and process until well combined. Add the pumpkin seeds to the mixture and briefly pulse just until combined.

Firmly press the mixture into the baking pan using a flat metal spatula to create a smooth, even layer. Place pan in the freezer for about an hour before cutting into eight bars.

Place in an airtight container and store in the refrigerator for up to one month.

POST-RACE MEAL RECIPE: CROCKPOT CHILI (SERVES 4)

1 lb. lean ground beef	2 Tbsp. chili powder
1 Tbsp. olive oil	2 tsp. cumin
3 cloves fresh garlic, minced	1 pinch cayenne pepper
2 large red bell peppers, seeded and diced	⅛ tsp. ground black pepper
	dash of salt
1 small onion, chopped	1 (28 oz.) can crushed tomatoes
4 stalks celery, chopped	2 Tbsp. tomato paste
1 large carrot, chopped	1 (15 oz.) can chili beans (pinto, kidney,
1 jalapeno pepper, chopped (optional)	and/or black beans, rinsed and drained)
1 Tbsp. chopped basil	Optional garnish: low-fat sour cream, yogurt, or shredded cheddar cheese

Sauté the garlic and onion in 1 tsp. olive oil over medium heat in a nonstick skillet until the garlic just begins to soften and brown. Add the ground beef and cook while stirring until the meat is browned. Transfer to a large clean bowl and set aside.

Add 2 tsp. olive oil to the pan and sauté the bell peppers, carrots, celery, and jalapeno pepper, and cook until softened (about five minutes). Stir in the chopped basil, and mix the vegetable mixture into the cooked meat. Sprinkle the spices onto the meat mixture and stir thoroughly.

In a slow cooker, mix together the tomatoes, tomato paste, beans, and the meat and vegetable mixture, and stir well.

Cover and cook on high setting for about four or five hours. Serve with a dollop of sour cream or a sprinkle of cheddar cheese and crackers on the side.

CONCLUSION

This chapter is not intended to sell anyone on any sweeping dietary imperatives or convince runners that the difference between themselves and a jump to national-class standing is a simple reformulation of their carbohydrate-protein-fat ratio. What's important is that young runners and their guides need to recognize when their nutrition, and thus their health, has started to suffer owing to obsessive habits that start small and blossom, outright eating disorders like anorexia and bulimia, and falling short of key micro- and macronutrients such as iron and protein as a result of these habits or of adopting a contemporary canned diet plan of any sort. Indeed, eating should be viewed as a pleasure, not a mere biochemical obligation. As young athletes mature, they will hopefully learn not only to fuel themselves properly to ensure optimal performance, but also to do this in a way that is fun, tasty, rewarding, and free of guilt. No one, athletic or otherwise, should feel compelled to apologize for what he or she eats, how this plays into his or her physical appearance, or how these things relate to their personal concept of wellness. Youngsters can get assistance with all of these things, but getting there starts and finishes with the same confidence, discipline, and self-assurance that are necessary to become successful as a runner overall.

6

THE ROLE OF A MENTOR

Mantra: *I am loved and supported*

A number of years ago, on an exceptionally warm September evening, Lize Brittin stood on a cross-country course directing children who were running half-mile, one-mile, or two-mile races. Parents were scattered about, clapping and cheering as these kids—all of them in grade school— ran by, some of them determined and focused, others smiling and laughing.

Programs such as the Land Sharks, a running club for kids in kindergarten through sixth grade in Boulder, Colorado, didn't exist when Lize was growing up in the 1970s and early 1980s. She found it heartwarming to see the support and guidance parents and coaches were offering to each and every youngster competing. The focus here was on participating, not winning.

This cheerful scene stood in obvious contrast to that described in a November 2012 *New York Times* article by Barry Bearak called "Too Fast, Too Soon." The article describes a father, Rodney Welsch, coaxing his daughters Kaytlynn, 12, and Heather, 10, into running a thirteen-mile trail race, a typical event for the two youngsters. Rodney Welsch, it is apparent, sees nothing wrong with the fact that Heather sometimes cries in races. He gives Kaytlynn a hard time for placing "only" sixth in one race. It's hard to imagine a parent not being thrilled for a child finishing so high—or for simply finishing such a challenging race. The main concern about these young girls is the impact that their intense training will have on their developing bodies, but there are also the mental and emotional aspects to consider. How will pushing them now affect them later in their running careers?

THE PUSHING-KIDS-TOO-HARD SYNDROME

It's necessary to look at why some parents feel the need to push a young child into any activity that's physically or psychologically taxing or intense, be it running, gymnastics, or beauty pageants. Maturity is an asset in the sport of running, so to prematurely place a child in a highly structured and competitive environment serves no logical purpose. It's possible that some parents who don't allow young athletes to progress at their own natural rates are trying to live vicariously through their children, perhaps allowing their own unrealized dreams to interfere with what their children really want and need. Barb Higgins, a teacher and highly successful running coach from New Hampshire, sums up the various perils of this kind of zealous leadership: "More than the obvious physical implications of racing long distances at a young age, I worry for their self-esteem and sense of self, period. Who are they if they aren't runners?" Higgins coached Rachel Umberger to a national 800-meter title in 2002, and her Concord High School girls were ranked eleventh in the nation in the year 2000 by *Harrier* magazine.

One of the potential physical problems of pushing a young runner is that excessive miles impose a major stress on a growing body. Too much repetitive pounding can lead to injuries. The growth plates in the bones of children are softer and more fragile than those of adults, so a demanding regimen carries an especially high risk of fractures. A parent who doesn't have coaching or running experience might not understand all aspects of the activity and might not be able to relate to the physical, emotional, and mental stress of this demanding sport. It's simply not necessary for young runners to be engaged with all aspects of the sport like a professional. Massage therapists, physical therapists, and extra coaching all have their place, but not necessarily in the life of a runner who is not yet or barely a teenager and just starting to explore the sport.

For young girls, a big concern is that too much focus on running can, in the absence of psychological support, predispose them to eating disorders. It can be difficult for coaches to understand that not everyone is capable of making choices that are in her best interest. If there is pressure to succeed, the child is at risk of "getting lost" and beginning to define herself in terms of her sport instead of finding her true self. As a result, she may increasingly isolate herself from peers, especially in the ever-present shadow of a parent overly invested in his daughter's performance. With too much training too early, young girls also experience a greater risk of the delayed onset of puberty. Boys and girls may need different approaches to training, recovery, and motivation, and a mentor cannot be afraid to address issues that arise from this reality, especially for young girls. In addition to addressing mental and emotional aspects, a mentor needs to be aware of physical concerns. Puberty affects boys and girls differently, and a coach must be educated on how these changes can affect his runners. When done in the right way, however, running can be a positive experience for youngsters.

A certain amount of pressure, applied effectively, can encourage younger competitors to rise to the challenge. But too much stress, especially at a young age, can lead to poor performance and other setbacks, including health troubles. Teaching kids to handle stressors in a healthy way generally leads to better performances, and handling stress constructively plays out not only in competition but in kids' everyday lives as well. In order to avoid "burnout," coaches need to give kids the leeway to be kids and not worry about the burdens of outcome-based running. Just like adults, children handle stress in a number of ways, and a coach needs to be aware of not only how each of his runners is affected in high-pressure situations, but also the best way to guide each individual through those situations.

One key factor in coaching is knowing how to respond when a runner is at the "moment of truth"—that point in a race at which fatigue has set in and the mind can begin to waver. How a coach reacts when his athletes reach the stage of a race when things become truly challenging, even painful, is crucial. Does he encourage his runners or does he yell? Does he come across as passionate or merely emotional? Again, boys and girls might respond differently, but most people, especially kids, don't react well to drill-sergeant tactics. Knowing that most kids operate better with positive feedback, a coach must find creative ways to encourage his runners. Statements such as "Stay strong and relaxed!" "Run beautifully!" and "Focus on your form!" will go much further than "Just do it!" "Everybody else is hurting too!" and "Push harder!" in producing healthy and successful runners. Every coach should adopt the motto "Train; don't strain."

THE COACH-RUNNER DYNAMIC

Melody Fairchild is a professional athlete and coach who directs running camps for girls in high school and middle school. One of the most valuable lessons she teaches young runners is to know what it is that makes them happy. This is important because it puts children on the path to self-awareness. Self-awareness is the anchor that allows runners to stay firmly on their feet and have the wisdom to know what is in their best interest. Communication between the brain and the body and body awareness are essential for anyone who wants to run well. Self-efficacy is a key ingredient in making a great competitor. Runners must know when their training isn't working and have a sense of when what their coaches are saying or doing isn't appropriate. Part of the process of becoming a healthy and successful runner is navigating both internal and external dialogues—that is, perceiving what's behind both the messages the mind is telling itself and the things coaches and others are saying. Instead of fleeing from an uncomfortable situation, learning to cope and handle challenges in a healthy manner can be beneficial and empowering.

Because some kids might see a coach as an authority figure, it can be hard for them to consider the idea that a coach, just like a teacher or parent, may not be perfect. Trusting the self is crucial in such a case, and part of the coach's job is to help runners build a strong sense of identity. Coaches may unknowingly or unconsciously become parental figures to the kids on the team, and this can create an unhealthy environment, especially (but not only) in cases where there is tumult in the home—issues which the coach may know nothing about. If a coach is too enmeshed with an individual, it can lead to undesirable patterns that involve the runner taking on too much responsibility and being unable to develop and maintain a firm sense of individuality. A coach who is overly committed to one or a few athletes will likely be unable to provide a training program that is sensible and suitable for everyone on the team.

Fairchild uses role-playing and "what if" scenarios to teach her kids how to be aware of what sounds sensible and how to effectively communicate with a coach. Both Higgins and Fairchild encourage runners to listen to their bodies. This translates into a strong sense of self-confidence that can help in all areas of life. Says Higgins, "Running and withstanding physical pain requires the ability to have long conversations with your body about why it should keep running even though it wants to stop." Mental toughness, she adds, is really just having an open communication with your body. Learning to trust your gut, your inner voice, is what communication and standing up for yourself comes down to. She feels that it's a good idea to have peers who act as mentors on the team as well because it's often easier to open up to someone who is the same age. Fairchild agrees and suggests that standout kids can make great leaders and role models for the other participants in the group.

Despite having won the Foot Locker National High School Cross Country Championship race twice, Fairchild never considered seeking additional help beyond her high-school coach. In addition to balking at the cost of hiring a private coach, Fairchild felt that it was important to be a 100-percent member of her high-school team. It was beneficial for her to experience a sense of camaraderie and esprit de corps. She wanted to build a relationship with her coach and believed that his philosophy about training was sound. With measurable improvements over the first years of training with him, she was convinced that her best option was to take the saying "Bloom where you are planted" to heart. The idea is to do the best you can with what you're given, and in Fairchild's case, she considers herself lucky to have had a solid coach.

In general, high-school coaches are well trained and dedicated to helping their kids reach their goals. If a problem arises or a runner feels that his training isn't helping him progress, it's essential to communicate about what isn't working and design alternatives. A good coach should be willing to listen to the needs of others. Nobody should be afraid to engage in a discussion with a mentor. Only when a situation seems unreasonable and the person in charge is unwilling to bend should the family consider hiring an outside coach. Although keeping stress to a minimum allows for better training conditions for any runner, part of becoming a good athlete is learning to deal with all kinds of situations, including difficult ones. When a youngster takes the initiative to undertake the process of conflict resolution, it can build her self-esteem, and learning to identify and express her needs early can improve her sense of self-efficacy.

The relationship between a coach and a runner should be strong while including appropriate boundaries. All runners on the team should be given ample, if not always equal, attention. There's no need for a coach to be spending hours outside of normal practice time with any runner. Even top runners don't need special treatment outside of the school program, and too much advice—however well-meaning—can be confusing to an athlete. In order for a coach to make training less stressful for her runners, it's essential to filter the input of outsiders. The best strategy is to focus on what the coach says. Parents and fans who may not really be qualified to offer suggestions have their place in a runner's life, but should not try to subsume the role of the coach; doing so will create a discordant atmosphere.

WHAT TO ASK A NEW COACH

- Why did the coach go into coaching kids?
- What are the coach's credentials?
- What is the coach's history in sport as a fan or a participant?
- Can the coach give some examples of past runners doing well under his or her plan?
- What is the coach's philosophy around training?
- Can the coach give a sample training program?
- What is the coach's availability?
- If hiring outside of a school setting, what does the coach charge?
- How does the coach keep things fun?
- How does the coach add variety into training programs, and how often does he or she suggest racing?

WHAT MAKES A TRULY GOOD MENTOR?

Too often, coaches fail to consider running's emotional aspects. The result can be a burned-out young runner saddled with injuries and frustration. It can be tempting for a coach or parent to want to push a young competitor who is clearly possessed of unusual talent, but long-term considerations should prevail. If a mentor can step back and learn to develop individuals at a reasonable rate, helping young runners identify their strengths rather than blindly exploiting their successes, then that mentor has done a good job. A common element among top runners is that they have learned to read their bodies and have discovered what they need in order to race well. By the time a runner reaches college, he should have a good sense of self-efficacy and should know what his body can and cannot handle in terms of mileage and hard sessions, at least at his current level of physical and athletic maturity.

Perhaps the biggest mistake that coaches make in training young runners is having them specialize too early. They often overemphasize interval training and workout times, and coaches and runners alike can fall prey to focusing solely on outcomes at the expense of appreciating and refining the training and competitive maturation process. A coach whose whole approach revolves around objective racing performance risks making bad decisions. At younger ages, a coach should teach general skills and the basics of running and worry less about place and time—concerns that, for the most part, can wait until high school. Attention to form with an emphasis on upper-body strength, posture, and arm position is important. Drills to improve stride and turnover are an excellent way to give younger runners the building blocks of becoming a well-rounded athlete. These are tools they can use throughout their entire careers, and in runners who have developed poor habits early on, small adjustments in form and improvements in coordination early can lead to profound results down the road.

Ultimately, the best coaches are those who don't seek personal validation from their runners' performances. They have no attachments to their runners' competitive exploits other than the desire to see them reach their dreams and sharing in their resulting satisfaction, and they understand that it takes a well-rounded and balanced individual to make a great competitor. In schools with a long history of winning big and the reputation that goes with it, expectations naturally run high. Unfortunately, some coaches' egos invariably become part of the mix, and they place self-interest and even certain social expectations above the well-being of their runners. An ego-driven coach is prone to making mistakes and typically winds up pushing his or her runners too hard or in the wrong direction.

A good coach needs to be flexible—willing and able to make changes to training schedules on the fly and sometimes at a moment's notice. Keeping the kids on a team healthy and helping them set and reach realistic goals is a challenge, but a combination of planning and adaptability makes it possible. Says Higgins, "Sometimes the mojo was more important than the scientific necessity of a particular workout on that particular day. If one of my runners was emotionally drained or physically struggling, I knew to alter the workout for the day. You have to look at the big picture. I kept a general blueprint for each week, but it was always fluid. I feel it's better to be undertrained than overtrained." In addition to building flexibility into your runners' running program, you should limit their racing to two or three seasons, with the summer typically set aside for training only. Year-round racing can lead to injuries and burnout, so a race-free block of time is vital, as is adequate downtime between seasons themselves (for example, a week or two off between the end of cross-country and the beginning of indoor track season). For most runners, building a base through mostly easy running during the off-season allows for more successful racing in subsequent months.

Scott Fry, winner of the 1984 Kinney National Cross-Country Championships (the predecessor of the Foot Locker series), focused very heavily on running as a teen. Though this clearly contributed to his high level of success, he doesn't recommend that others take the same path. "I wouldn't have changed a thing in high school other than give some more thought to life beyond running," he says today. "I basically put it all into running. It worked out well for me. I got a full-ride scholarship and had a lot of great experiences." Fry adds, however, that he would not want his son or any runners he coaches to become so singularly focused on what is likely to be a comparatively short part of their lives—most runners don't compete at a high level after college if they continue racing at all. Indeed, high-performing runners who avoid putting all of their eggs in one basket, remaining highly committed without becoming one-dimensional, are actually more likely to have longer and more successful running careers. Fairchild offers a perfect example of someone finding this balance and achieving great long-term success, and she's not alone. Alan and Shayne Culpepper were both world-class runners in the 1990s when they formed their graphic-design business, Culpepper Mill, and in 2010, two-time U.S. 5,000-meter champion Lauren Fleshman founded her own energy-bar company.

Sometimes a coach's job isn't just to supervise runners in workouts or to prepare racers for an upcoming event, but also to guide troubled individuals to more solid ground. A coach using the "come back and see me when you're running well" approach usually won't produce great runners, but unfortunately, many coaches operate this way anyway. In order to optimally tackle a serious fitness and conditioning plan, a runner needs to be in good working order on all levels, not just physically. The "person first, athlete second" idea is one that many coaches fail to grasp or accept. As long as a competitor is running well, this sort of coach gives him the attention and support he needs, but might subtly abandon him when he becomes injured or races poorly. Even the best runners are rarely taught how to weather the uncomfortable feelings of frustration and helplessness that often arise during periods of injury or other unplanned downtime, but it's essential to help runners learn to manage these difficult times in order to achieve long-term running success. A competent and compassionate coach stands by her runners when they are struggling mightily, when they are on top of the world, and at all times in between. Want for them what you would want for yourself or your own children.

7

THE BREAKDOWN LANE

Mantra: *I can do this*

One of the biggest roles of a coach is to offer support and guidance to an athlete who is injured, sick, or overtrained. Many coaches don't know how to guide an athlete successfully through times when injury or illness strikes—especially when the timing is especially poor. It's easier to be supportive when an athlete is training and running well, but facing an injury can be one of the most difficult situations for a young runner, and virtually every runner becomes hurt at some point.

It's essential to rest an injury, but certain injuries allow for some cross-training. The key is to try to avoid losing too much fitness while healing and recovering. It's better to risk losing some fitness, though, if it means getting back to running at 100 percent more quickly.

COMMON INJURIES

Most injuries that occur in young runners are the result of the mechanical stress of repetitive motion to which not-yet-fully-mature joints and tissues are subjected. Running on soft surfaces can help ease some of the pounding on the body, but it takes more than carefully choosing where to run to stay healthy. In other sports, such as basketball or soccer, athletes are at risk for acute injuries from physical contact or falls. However, in running, the more prevalent threat comes in the form of chronic injuries from overuse or overtraining (the occasional sprained ankle or other traumatic event notwithstanding). Young runners are particularly at risk for these types of injuries because their bodies are still developing. Early identification of the injury, informed treatment, and training modifications are essential for reducing recovery time and preventing any serious complications.

RUNNING FORM BASICS

Fast cadence
Forward lean
Upper body shoulders down
Arm posture with hands that don't drop below waist
Quick and efficient arm swing
Powerful foot landing
Relaxed upper body
High heel lift in back
Knee raised up to create forward momentum
Do what's comfortable for your body

One very common injury in high-school runners—and new runners of all ages—is *shin splints*. This type of injury is a stress reaction that's seen more commonly in novice runners and almost always occurs bilaterally. While the injury itself isn't considered to be that serious in terms of pure physical damage, the pain that an athlete experiences can be significant. Left untreated, shin splints can become debilitating for a young athlete and can potentially develop into stress fractures. According to Dr. Richey Hansen, there's no way to accurately determine which athletes will end up with a stress fracture once they are diagnosed with shin splints, so it's best to treat every case prudently. Officially called "medial tibial stress," shin splints can be caused by a number of factors, such as running too much on hard surfaces, having tight calves, or overpronating (rolling the feet inward), but typically the injury is seen more in athletes who increase their volume and intensity of training too quickly. In newcomers, virtually any amount of running can translate to "too much, too soon," leaving these runners especially susceptible.

With the right treatment and precautions, it's fairly easy to keep this injury under control. The first step is to identify and correct the injury by changing the running surface to primarily soft surfaces, using adequate footwear including shoe inserts if necessary, and treating tight calves by gently stretching. You can keep the symptoms at bay by using a regimen of ice, rest, and, eventually, a gradual reintroduction to training, making sure to alternate running days with non-weight-bearing exercise days until there is no sign of the pain returning.

It must be noted that to some extent, getting past the pain of shin splints for some people requires training through the injury, lightly and prudently; backing off completely at the first sign of pain often results in the shin splints reasserting themselves after the rest period ends. Clearly, this behavior, if judged to be the wisest course of action, must be very carefully monitored.

Another common malady among runners, especially high-mileage types, is *stress fractures*. As opposed to shin splints, this injury is a lot more serious and can even result in a full bone fracture if left untreated. Young athletes go through a period in which their bones grow and develop. The consistent stress of some 1,500 foot strikes per mile can damage the bone, especially when the muscles near and around the bone become fatigued and aren't able to absorb additional shock. Over time, as the muscles transfer the workload onto the bone, the bone begins to break down.

Most stress fractures in young athletes occur in the bones of the lower legs or feet, but some can occur in the hips and pelvis. The strongest predictor of stress fractures in young runners is a history of previous stress fractures, bone breaks, and other bone issues, a finding that sheds light on the fact that many coaches fail to take necessary training precautions with young athletes and apprise themselves of their runners' histories. Typically, a fracture won't occur twice in the same place on the bone because the bony callus that forms during the healing process actually results in the fracture site being unusually resilient. But a single bone—most often the tibia, or shin bone—can sustain multiple fractures months or even years apart.

The best treatment once a stress fracture is detected is complete rest for at least two weeks and very light, non-weight-bearing exercises for another four to six weeks. Dr. Hansen advises his patients to take six to eight weeks off if the stress fracture occurs in the femur (thigh bone), the largest bone in the body. He also notes that it's important to make sure the diet isn't lacking in calcium, calories, and overall nutrition during the healing phase.

In the past, doctors completely immobilized a stress fracture in a plaster cast, but depending on the location of the injury, many doctors today will prescribe a walking cast or air cast instead. As long as weight is kept off the injury to the fullest extent possible, this will let the bone heal while allowing for some mobility, which, in turn, will keep the muscles around the injury from significantly atrophying.

As a rule, any exercise done during recovery should be non-weight-bearing. Ultimately, the best approach is to monitor training loads in order to prevent the chance of a stress fracture ever occurring.

Runner's knee, as the name implies, is seen most often in running versus other sports but can develop in anyone who participates in activities that require a lot of bending of the knees. The term actually refers to a mélange of ailments, all affecting the area where the patella meets the top of the tibia (shin bone) beneath it. The most telling symptom is pain behind or under the kneecap during activity.

Because there are no clearly defined precipitating factors, such as structural abnormalities or bone damage, runner's knee can be hard to treat. Runner's knee can be related to patellar tendonitis, bursitis, and chondromalacia. Strengthening exercises such as leg extensions on gym machines for the quadriceps (thigh) muscles and the muscles around the knee such as the vastus medialis and vastus lateralis muscles can help stabilize the knee and lower body and prevent the patella from grinding against the top of the tibia. With no discernible physical issue to treat, however, doctors have more recently favored treating the pain itself. Ultimately, the best approach is to treat the pain using physician-guided doses of anti-inflammatory medications such as ibuprofen while working to see if you can trace the problem to a postural issue, gait issue, or muscle weakness.

While muscle tears are generally seen more frequently in sprinters and older athletes, nearly all athletes are at risk for muscle strains. *Strains* occur in the muscles, while *sprains* occur in the ligaments. Runners are especially at risk for straining hamstring, quadriceps, and calf muscles. If a muscle or ligament is overstretched, micro-tears can develop, and the result is usually pain, weakness, and inflammation. If the pull or micro-tears develop into a full-blown tear or rupture, surgery might be required. For less serious conditions, two weeks with a regimen of rest or scaling back activity, ice, compression, and elevation are recommended. Later, mobility, strengthening, and range of motion exercises should be added along with some professional massage therapy to reduce the risk of reinjury. Start back to running very gradually, making sure to slowly increase volume before adding any kind of intensity.

If you're going to take a stand, you need your feet. If you're going to create an odyssey, you need sound feet. Unfortunately, running is hard on the feet, and foot injuries will bring an athlete to a halt.

Plantar fasciitis is an inflammation or, in extreme cases, a tear of the plantar fascia, the ligament that consists of a thick band of tissue at the bottom of the feet. The band supports the arch of the foot and extends from the heel to the toes. When the ligament becomes inflamed due to overtraining, poor biomechanics, tight calf muscles, worn-out shoes, high-heeled shoes, or running too many hard workouts on hard surfaces, pain radiates from the heel throughout the bottom of the foot. The pain is usually worse in the morning, especially when taking your first steps after getting out of bed.

For serious cases, Hansen suggests wearing a walking boot to remove any stress on the foot for at least a week, longer for stubborn cases that heal more slowly. During cross-training activities, the boot can be removed, but all exercises should be non-weight-bearing as the injury heals. Once the athlete is pain free, loaded squats, calf stretches, and a slow return to usual activity can be added to her training regimen.

The Achilles tendon or calcaneal tendon is the longest tendon in the body. It runs from the lower end of the calf all the way down to the back of the heel bone. With repetitive activity such as running, especially running with any kind of intensity, the tendon can become irritated. Symptoms of Achilles tendonitis include pain, swelling, and limited range of motion in the ankle, especially when flexing and extending the foot. Since the tendon itself doesn't contain a generous blood supply, swelling usually occurs in the tissue surrounding the tendon. Injury to the tendon can range from a full rupture to mild irritation. Most cases of tendonitis can be treated with non-surgical methods, but surgery is a consideration if the condition becomes chronic or the tendon is torn or ruptured.

Non-surgical treatments include immobilizing the lower leg by using a heel lift inserted into the shoe, icing the painful area, resting, and very light stretching. A doctor might suggest wearing an air cast and taking anti-inflammatory medications for at least two weeks in more severe cases. The key to recovery when dealing with Achilles tendonitis is patience. Often, runners will feel a reduction in pain after a limited amount of rest and try to return to full activity too quickly. This will only cause the tendon to become irritated again. An athlete should wait until there is no pain in the affected area and then wait another week or two before very gradually reintroducing normal activity.

The iliotibial band consists of fasciae that form a thick band that surrounds the muscles on the outside of the thigh, connecting the hip muscles to the tibia. *Iliotibial band syndrome* (ITBS) is usually caused by ineffective muscle control and improper coordination in the hip. The result is that the band that moves over the outside of the femoral epicondyle doesn't work as efficiently as it should and ends up getting stretched or irritated. Symptoms include lateral knee pain; swelling along the outside of the knee; tightness; burning or stinging sensations from the outside of the hip to the knee; and a snapping sensation over the knee as it bends or straightens.

Hansen suggests exercises such as plyometrics and loaded plyometrics to improve stability, coordination, strength, and motor control, especially in the hip. Proper coordination and strength will prevent the knee from rotating, and this will keep the iliotibial band from becoming irritated or overstretched. As with other injuries, running should be avoided when there is intense pain. Once the area has calmed down, and the pain is gone or nearly gone, athletes can add some easy running, working on volume before any intensity is added back to the program.

NUTRITION: WHAT TO KEEP IN MIND WHEN INJURED

- Calcium: Green leafy vegetables, dairy products, sesame seeds, edamame, and oranges
- Boron: Black beans, artichokes, figs, walnuts, avocadoes, and prunes
- Vitamin D: Salmon, tuna, sardines, fortified milk, egg yolks, and beef liver
- Magnesium: Spinach, pumpkin seeds, almonds, yogurt, bananas, and figs
- Iron: Chicken or beef liver, oysters, red meat, chicken, sardines, and turkey (non-heme iron sources found in plants such as spinach are not as absorbable)
- Foods to boost serotonin: Sweet potatoes, cheese, eggs, pineapple, salmon, almonds, and tofu
- Fiber: Figs, green leafy vegetables, whole grains, berries, avocadoes, and acorn squash
- Vitamin B-rich foods: Beef liver, fortified cereals, salmon, brewer's yeast, and turnip greens
- Essential Fatty Acids: Fish oil, flaxseed oil, chia seeds, butternuts, walnuts, and tuna
- Vitamin C: Oranges, kale, peppers, guava, berries, tomatoes, and peas

INJURY PREVENTION

One of the most effective ways to deal with injuries is to take measures to prevent them from happening in the first place. By dedicating a small amount of time to recovery exercises in a training regimen, you can greatly lower the chances of injuries popping up.

Some of the biggest reasons young athletes get injured are that they either lack enough fuel and nutrition for their workload or aren't properly recovering, or they are not properly managing the volume and intensity of their workouts. These risk factors can be mitigated by implementing a sound diet, building strength, and getting enough quality sleep—ideally, eight hours or so at night. Naps within a few hours after hard workouts or races can also be beneficial, as sleep in general helps decrease cortisol levels, promotes recovery, and aids in healthy metabolism. Adolescents require more sleep than adults.

Using treatment tools such as ice, self-massage, and foam rollers on sore or nagging areas can reduce the chance of minor aches and pains developing into serious injuries as long as you don't aggravate an already inflamed area through overzealous use of these self-treatments. Cross-training (see chapter 8) is also a very effective way to address an injury before it develops into a season-ending issue. If pain is consistent and isn't responding to the treatments, substitute biking, pool running, or elliptical sessions for a few days of running. These options will give the body a reprieve from the consistent pounding caused by running while still giving an aerobic benefit to the athlete, especially one who competes in states offering indoor track as a formal varsity sport.

Another major topic of discussion among high-school coaches and athletes is how much time to take off between competitive seasons. Some say two weeks between seasons is sufficient, while others will allow their athletes a longer break. While there isn't necessarily a magic number, most coaches would agree that athletes need a very distinct off-season in which they aren't running at all. That doesn't mean that they can't engage in other physical activities during this time. However, young athletes need time completely away from the sport and the physical demands it places on their bodies. Even the top Kenyan marathoners, among the best distance runners the world has ever known, reportedly take up to an entire month off from running once the competitive season is over.

ACTIVITIES ON A REST DAY

Leisure swimming
Bike to a picnic
Take a short stroll or easy hike with a friend
Curl up with a hot cup of tea and a good book
Get a relaxing massage
Do some light yoga
Take a nap
Set some goals
Stretch and do some foam rolling
Do a short and easy weightlifting session

IMMEDIATE INJURY CARE

The type of immediate care an injury needs naturally depends on the nature of the problem. Treatment can include hot, cold, or alternating hot-and-cold compresses; ice; elevation of the affected area; and, of course, rest. Sometimes, a doctor will suggest taking a nonsteroidal anti-inflammatory drug (NSAID) such as Aleve (naproxen sodium) or Advil (ibuprofen) on a temporary basis. For more severe injuries, visiting a doctor is your best bet.

If you suspect the presence of a stress fracture, schedule a doctor's visit for your athlete right away. Confirmation of such injury usually requires an X-ray, MRI, or bone scan. Since this is not an injury you want to risk making worse, it's better to immediately get looked at by a professional. Stress fractures typically require at least six weeks of complete rest while the bone remodels, so getting an early diagnosis rather than waiting and seeing how the injury fares will shorten the overall recovery time.

If the injury seems to be more related to soft tissue (i.e., muscles and fasciae), seeing a massage therapist or physical therapist can usually provide almost immediate relief. More serious issues may require consistent treatment over a period of days, weeks, or even months, but many issues can be resolved with aggressive initial treatment as soon as you are aware of any abnormal or lingering pain.

LONG-TERM INJURY CARE

Recurring injuries often indicate the presence of a biomechanical or structural issue. Many times, these issues can be corrected with strength training or treatment by a physical therapist. Athletes who have dealt with multiple problems can benefit greatly from working with a specialist trained in recognizing and identifying muscle or structural weaknesses. Treatment plans will usually involve corrective exercises and potentially include the use of custom orthotic shoe inserts.

ILLNESS AND SICKNESS

Running when sick generally isn't a good idea. Any activity more than a gentle walk or bike ride will generally make symptoms of a cold or other illness worse. Take some downtime if you are fighting an illness, and be gentle with yourself as you step back into training. It's best to wait a day after you experience your last symptom before you begin training again, but sometimes runners, being highly motivated creatures by constitution, are impatient and want to start back as soon as possible.

As long as there is no indication of fever, Brad suggests the twenty-minute rule to determine whether athletes should continue training when there's a question regarding their health. Do not run at all if you have a fever, the flu, or a respiratory infection, and don't continue if, after a few minutes, you experience any serious symptoms, such as dizziness or intense pain. If you are unsure about whether or not to go for a bona fide training run, give it a go for twenty minutes to see if you are truly up to the task. It's best to do two ten-minute laps, so that if you are really not feeling well, you can stop early in the same place you started. Generally, it takes at least ten to twenty minutes for your body to warm up, even under optimal conditions, so the goal is to get through that in order to decide if you're feeling like you should continue. Often, even when you're not feeling 100 percent, a short jog can actually make you feel better. Warming up for twenty minutes can help you determine if running will make you feel better or worse that day.

Common Cold vs. Influenza

The symptoms of the common cold are usually milder than those of influenza or the flu. Congestion, a cough, headaches, and a sore throat might develop with a cold. The flu is a more serious illness than a cold that can turn into even more serious health issues such as pneumonia. A fever almost always accompanies the flu, and the symptoms are generally more severe, come on more quickly, and last longer than those of a cold. Body aches, weakness, vomiting, and diarrhea are signs of the flu.

With either illness, avoid running until you are no longer fatigued. It's more important to rest than to try to train when your body is already weakened and tired. Only if the symptoms are mild should you engage in some easy activity. In this case, raising the body temperature can actually be beneficial when it comes to fighting a cold, but you should avoid all hard workouts until you feel recovered.

SUCCESSFUL RETURN TO TRAINING

Starting back running after an injury or illness can be tricky. Most runners are anxious to get back into a routine of working out, but it's important to avoid running too far or too hard right away. Take the time to slowly build back into running by working on rebuilding an endurance base—competition and hard workouts can wait. With younger runners, even consistently running at an easy pace for eight weeks will lead to improvement.

Many coaches will use a run/walk method of training initially to build strength before even suggesting running after an injury or illness. Start out walking for five minutes, then jog for two, alternating walking with jogging until you have reached a total of twenty-five minutes. Add more running time each day as long as there is no sign of any pain or symptoms returning.

EMOTIONAL EFFECT OF INJURY

For an athlete, enduring an injury can be emotionally difficult. Running produces endorphins, so when you're not getting a dose of those feel-good chemicals in your brain from running, you have to find healthy ways to compensate. Keep calm. Keep your focus in the moment. Everything is easier to address and handle when your attention is on where you are, not where you want to be or where you were. You will heal more comfortably and possibly faster if you keep a positive attitude. Try not to get caught up in the "what ifs" and missed workouts and races. For a coach, be sure you watch for any signs of depression, such as loss in interest in everyday activities, changes in sleep patterns or eating habits, increased fatigue, trouble concentrating, or thoughts of self-harm, which you may have to ask about since very few people volunteer such information. Have your youngster see her physician if she experiences any of these symptoms.

Brad notes that a coach or mentor needs to give an injured athlete just as much attention and guidance as he would when she is healthy and running well. It's essential to give an athlete dealing with a setback as much support as possible, and a good coach can provide an injured runner a cross-training schedule. During times of injury, it can be a good idea to work on building overall strength by lifting weights. With many injuries, it's safe to keep training aerobically by swimming, cycling, or using the elliptical machine, as long as these exercises don't aggravate the injury. These days, injured runners have more options than they did in the past and can use the Alter-G treadmill, pool vests when running in the water, or underwater treadmills.

The main goal when sick or injured should be on healing. Your runner's job is to get healthy. Everything else will fall into place later, so try to have patience. It's okay, even productive, for runners to imagine themselves running and continue dreaming about their running goals, and even write some of these goals out, but keep coming back to their overall health. Runners don't just want to run; they want to run well and to the best of their ability. This means they have to be healthy.

When dealing with an injury, it's a good time for people to catch up on things they might have let slide while they were putting more time and energy into training. They might try something new or catch up on reading or watching movies or put added energy into schoolwork. They can reconnect with or make more time for friends and remain a part of the team by going to practice in a supportive role, to cheer for others or help the coach time intervals. This will help your athlete feel connected. Mostly, though, athletes must allow themselves the rest their bodies need while they recover.

8

CROSS-TRAINING

Mantra: *My life, my rules*

We feel that to some extent, the term "cross-training" is inappropriate because it semantically devalues the work an athlete who presently can't run may be doing to maintain or even bolster fitness. While it's obviously true that runners, all else being equal, would generally prefer to be running, other aerobic activities such as cycling, swimming, aqua-running, cross-country skiing, rowing, and using an elliptical trainer are valuable in their own right and often enjoy a place in the regimens of even the most injury-resistant runners.

Cross-training is simply another form of training. It is not an activity that should be reserved solely for the injured runner. Cross-training can help athletes build a stronger foundation while reducing their risk of getting hurt and ultimately become better runners.

Despite the idea that training should be specific to your sport, running is a hard activity, and all the pounding limits what the body can withstand. Unlike cycling or swimming, sports in which athletes can participate for long periods of time, everyday runners can't typically train more than an hour or so at a time. Even the top marathoners in the world rarely exceed an average of about two hours a day. Splitting up runs in "two-a-days" or "doubles" can help reduce the repetitive stress somewhat, but it's not as much of a relief as engaging in non-weight-bearing exercises.

INJURY PREVENTION, REDUX

To build on the information in the previous chapter, while injury prevention is not the only reason to implement cross-training, it is certainly one of the most obvious. Running, by definition, requires repetitive motion for long periods of time, usually daily or almost daily. It is the very act of performing the same steps over and over, at a rate of about 180 steps per minute. It's no surprise that doing so will eventually take a toll on the body's bones and joints. Cross-training allows muscles and joints to be loaded in a different way without compromising the aerobic benefits of the exercise. Being injured doesn't have to mean being completely sidelined. If an athlete is experiencing pain or discomfort, replacing training runs a few days each week with cross-training can allow the body to heal and fend off a more serious injury.

It also shouldn't be assumed that an athlete has to be in pain to use cross-training for injury prevention. If you are working with someone who has experienced multiple injuries in the past, supplementing some portion of training with cross-training can be effective in preventing the same or related injuries from recurring. An anecdote concerning a colleague of former two-time Olympic marathoner and current Brigham Young University coach Ed Eyestone declares that the proper amount of mileage for an individual is to run as few miles as you can and still win. The moral of the story is that excessive "junk" or "garbage" miles are unnecessary and don't contribute to improved performance, but it takes a fair amount of low-intensity training in order to achieve aerobic conditioning, especially for longer events. There's a fine line between doing the right amount and going overboard. Some athletes, however, simply can't handle a lot of weekly miles, even highly gifted ones. As an athlete discovers what mileage produces the maximum potential for improvement without leading to setbacks, he or she may wish to incorporate non-running activities to further improve fitness without risking injury.

MOBILITY EXERCISES

For all mobility exercises, do six to ten repetitions on each leg once a day.

Hip Rotations

Have your athlete kneel on all fours with his hands squarely beneath his shoulders and his knees below his hips. His knees should be bent in the same 90-degree angle. Instruct him to rotate one leg around in a forward circle. After six to eight repetitions, have him rotate the leg in backward circles before switching legs.

Quadruped Hip Extension with Knee Bent

Instruct your athlete to kneel on all fours keeping a flat back with her hands squarely beneath her shoulders and her knees below her hips. Her fingers should be pointing forward and her feet pointing toward the wall behind her. Have her maintain a strong, stable core throughout the entire exercise and instruct her to engage her glute muscles as she lifts one leg up behind her, keeping her knee bent and raising her foot toward the ceiling. She should move only at the hip joint. Her knee, hip, and shoulder should all be even with her knee bent at about 90 degrees and her foot in the air above. Be sure she does the exercise on both legs.

Side Leg Lifts

Have your athlete begin by lying on one side with his body in a straight line from head to toe and his hips stacked directly on top of each other. He can prop himself up on his elbow. He should keep his leg straight as he lifts his top leg toward the ceiling and then slowly returns it to the starting position. You may want to tell him to lie with his back against a wall to make sure that he doesn't rotate his hips during this exercise. Have him perform the exercise on the opposite leg when done.

Ankle Stretch

Have your athlete sit in a chair and instruct him to use his big toe to write the alphabet in the air. Follow this with several ankle circles, first in one direction and then the other. End by having him flex and then point his foot.

Clamshells

For this exercise, your athlete will lie on the floor on one side with her knees bent at about 90 degrees. Make sure she keeps her body straight from her shoulder to her hip. Have her angle her thighs out in front of her body at about 135 degrees. She should keep her hips in alignment and engage her glutes as she brings the knee of her top leg up, opening her legs like a clamshell while keeping her ankles together.

Iron Cross

Have your athlete lie on her back with her arms out to her sides. She should keep her leg straight and her shoulders and upper back as flat against the floor as possible as she slightly rotates her hips and swings her left leg across her body and up to her right hand. Repeat the exercise for the opposite leg.

Lying Hip Rotations

Tell your athlete to lie on his back with his knees bent at a 90-degree angle. Have him place one leg over the other, right above the knee on the lower thigh. Instruct him to use his hand to gently push the knee of the leg on top away from his body. Have him bring his knee back to the starting position and repeat. Be sure to switch sides.

Glute Bridge

Instruct your athlete to lie down on her back on the floor with her knees bent at 90-degree angles. Her feet should be flat on the ground and about hip-width apart. She can rest her arms on the ground, but be sure she doesn't use them during the exercise. The exercise should target her glutes. Have her drive up through her heels to lift her hips off the ground. Tell her to push her hips up as high as possible, squeezing the glutes as she does so. Make sure she knows to engage her core as well. After she holds the pose for a few seconds, she can lower her hips back down to the ground and repeat eight times.

Squats

Have your athlete start in a standing position with his knees very slightly bent and his feet beneath his hips with his toes pointing forward. Make sure his posture is upright and that he engages his core. Have him hold his arms straight out in front of him with a slight bend in his elbows and the palms of his hands facing down. Instruct him to bend his knees and slowly and evenly lower himself down as if he were about to sit in a chair, until the tops of his thighs are parallel to the ground. Tell him to push his bottom out slightly as he moves into position and then raises himself back up to standing. Eventually, once he is comfortable with regular squats, he can add weights.

One-Legged Squat

Instruct your athlete to start in a standing position with her knees very slightly bent and her feet beneath her hips. Tell her to lift up her right leg and bend her knee slightly, just to get her foot off the ground. Have her hold her raised foot slightly behind her for the duration of the exercise. Using her left leg, she will lower herself into a squat position, keeping her hands slightly out in front of her for balance. To finish the exercise, she will return to an upright position. Have her repeat the exercise on the left side.

REHABILITATION

Even with the right precautions in place, there is always the possibility that injury will occur in running. You would be hard-pressed to find a top-level runner who hasn't been sidelined at least once with a significant injury. When running isn't an option due to injury, cross-training can be used not only as a way to both maintain and gain fitness, but also as a form of rehabilitation as well as stress relief. When dealing with specific injuries, some cross-training activities are more effective than others in terms of allowing the injury to heal. For example, pain in the Achilles tendon is going to be worsened by loading the foot, so cycling is a great alternative, as the foot remains relatively fixed (i.e., neither flexed nor extended) during the entirety of the workout. As obvious as it may sound, the best method is to monitor how a given injury responds to different types of cross-training and determine what modality causes the least amount of pain or discomfort both during and after the workout. In general, though, don't test the injury with exercises that seem intuitively contrary to healing. When in doubt, rest first, then use the pool before other kinds of exercise. Gradually, move along to other types of activity as the injury heals.

Running can be regarded as a linear sport. With little to no side-to-side motion, certain muscles are neglected. Not only does running place repetitive stress on muscles, bones, and joints, but it also can cause unused muscles to weaken. The problem that can occur when one muscle or muscle group in a pair (such as the quads and hamstrings) is strong and the opposing muscle is weak is called a neuromuscular imbalance. The muscle that is referred to as weak is actually remaining too relaxed when contracted and not necessarily weak, though it can feel like a weakness. In response to this relaxed state, the opposing muscle will contract more than it should. These types of imbalances can lead to postural irregularities and biomechanical problems that can cause further injury. Cross-training can assist with correcting any imbalances or inconsistencies by encouraging the body to work in different ways, incorporating other muscles and muscle groups. Doing so can strengthen weaknesses in the kinetic chain and not only help to rehabilitate injuries, but also prevent them from recurring. The idea is that a chain is only as strong as its weakest link, so strengthening any part of the weak chain will lead to improved health and performance.

STRENGTH TRAINING FOR RUNNERS

Plank

Have your athlete start by getting into push-up position on the floor. Instruct him to bend his elbows 90 degrees and rest his weight on his forearms with his forearms straight out. You might want to suggest that he make a fist with both hands. His elbows should be directly beneath his shoulders. His core should be engaged as much as possible throughout the exercise, and his body should be in a straight line from his head to his feet. As he holds the position, have him imagine pulling his elbows toward his feet without actually moving them. This will help him keep his core engaged. Make sure his back is flat. Have him hold the position for thirty seconds and work up to longer periods.

Side Planks

Have your athlete lie on the floor on her left side in a straight line. She should be propped up on her forearm. Her body should be straight with her elbow directly under her shoulder. For this exercise, she will have to have her core engaged as she gently lifts her hips straight up toward the ceiling, keeping her body as straight as possible with her hips square and her neck in line with her spine. Have her hold the peak position for about thirty seconds before lowering herself back down, still keeping her body in a straight line. Repeat two to three times, alternating sides. If this is too challenging, she can start with he knees bent at a 90-degree angle, so that instead of her feet being the main contact point on the floor, the knee of the leg on the bottom will be. For an extra challenge, she can try doing the exercise putting her weight on her hand with her arm straight instead of propping herself up on her forearm.

Push-ups

Instruct your athlete to start by lying on the floor on his stomach. Have him place his hands firmly on the ground directly under his shoulders with his body straight in a line, as he lifts himself up, so that his toes are supporting his lower half, while his hands support his upper body. Make sure he is engaging his core to keep his stomach from sagging down, his body straight, and his back flat. Have him slowly lower his body holding good form with his eyes focused about three feet in front of him until his chest barely touches the floor. At this point, he can push his body back up, still keeping his core engaged and his bottom flat, not pointing up, until he is back to the starting position. If this is too difficult, he can drop his knees to the ground instead of balancing on his toes. Have him start with ten repetitions and work up to three sets of ten.

Toe Raisers

Instruct your athlete to stand up straight with her feet hip-width apart and her knees ever so slightly bent. If she is worried about balance, she can hold onto the back of a chair during the exercise. Making sure your athlete is putting equal weight on each foot, have her slowly rise up onto the balls of her feet. At the peak position, she should engage her glute muscles in addition to her calf muscles, and then she can slowly lower herself back down, making sure her heels touch the ground. Repeat six times. She can also try these with one foot at a time.

Superman

Have your athlete lie down on the floor on his stomach with his arms extended out in front of him and his legs extended behind. His toes should be pointed toward the wall behind him, while his fingers point to the wall in front. Make sure he engages his core and his glute muscles, and in one movement, have him lift both his arms and legs up toward the ceiling, mimicking Superman flying in the sky. When done correctly, this will be a challenging exercise, so have him start by holding the position for five to ten seconds before he lowers his arms and legs back down to complete one repetition. In time, he can increase his repetitions from one to five.

Leg Curls

Leg curls can be done at the gym on a machine, but one can also do them at home. Instruct your athlete to stand facing a wall, or she can use the back of a chair for balance, with her feet below her hips and her toes pointing toward the wall. She can use ankle weights or a Thera-band eventually, but have her start without any added weight. Make sure her supporting leg is straight without the knee being locked. Have her place her hands on the wall or the chair for balance, and then flex her left knee, bringing her heel up toward her buttocks as far as she can making sure she keeps her body in alignment. After she holds the peak position for a few seconds, she can slowly bring her leg back down to the starting position and then repeat the curl with her right leg. Have her continue alternating legs for about ten repetitions on each leg.

Dead Lift

When your athlete begins this exercise, the barbell will be sitting on the floor. Have him approach the bar and stand with his shins right up against it and his feet just under the bar. His feet should stay parallel with each other throughout the entire exercise. Instruct him to grab the bar, each hand just outside of where his shins meet the bar. He should use an overhand grip and lock his elbows in a straight position. At the start, he will roll his shoulders back and look straight ahead, so that his chest is open while he pushes his weight to the back, leaning until his toes almost come up off the ground. He will want to engage his glutes throughout this exercise. As he lifts the bar off the ground, he should keep it close to his body until he is standing upright with his arms hanging down. Make sure his back is flat as he lifts. He should use the same form as he slowly lowers the bar back down. Have him start out with six repetitions using just the bar before adding weights to it.

Crunches

Instruct your athlete to begin by lying flat on a mat. Have her lift her legs up, so that both her knees and her hips are at a 90-degree angle. Her lower legs will be parallel with the ground. Have her place her arms straight down by her sides on the ground with her fingers pointing toward her feet. Before she starts the crunch, have her take a breath in, and as she lifts her upper torso up off the floor, tell her to stretch her arms in the direction of her feet and exhale. From there, she can slowly inhale again as she gently lowers herself back down. Have her complete one set of ten repetitions, and add an additional set every one to two weeks until she can complete three sets of ten.

Step-ups

Your athlete will need to use a wide step, a Plyometrics Box, a very stable short chair, or a stable bench for this exercise. Ideally, his knee will be bent at about a 90-degree angle when he steps up on it. Have him start with his left foot, and instruct him to set it up onto the step, making sure his entire foot is safely and securely planted. Then he will lift his right foot up, pressing through the heel and rolling up off the toe as he steps onto the bench, bringing his right foot up to meet the left on the step. He will be standing on the step briefly before lowering his right foot back down to the ground. Then, have him bring his left foot down to meet his right on the ground to complete one repetition. He should complete ten full steps leading with the left foot before switching to the right foot leading the exercise. When this becomes too easy for him, he can hold dumbbells in his hands for the duration of the exercise.

One-Legged Overhead Dumbbell Press

Have your athlete start out using 5-lb. dumbbells in each hand. If this becomes too easy, she can always add weight. First, have her stand with both feet on the ground with her feet directly below her hips and her back in a neutral position. To begin, she will bend one knee, so that her leg is raised slightly off the floor in front of her with her foot at least a few inches off the ground. Her supporting leg should be straight but not locked at the knee. Have her hold the dumbbells up near her ears. The dumbbells should be parallel to the wall behind her, and the palms of her hands should be facing forward. She can then slowly lift both weights from the height of her shoulders up toward the ceiling until her arms are straight and then slowly return the weights to the starting position. Complete six to eight repetitions and then switch legs.

SUPPLEMENTARY TRAINING

Even if an athlete doesn't have a history of injury susceptibility, cross-training can be integrated into training to increase the amount of time spent on aerobic development without increasing the weight-bearing stress load put on a young athlete's developing body. You can add cross-training to a training schedule in two general ways: you can add it in place of an easy run or as a hard effort in place of a structured or interval workout. It's usually more effective to use a heart-rate monitor during such workouts since you obviously can't use pace as a gauge as you would when running. The goal of supplementary workouts is simply to mimic the aerobic efforts derived from running without putting the same biomechanical stress on the body. Some of the most common exercises used to supplement training are cycling, pool running, or using the elliptical machine. Some people will even use a stand-up method on the stationary bike to more closely mimic running.

COMPLEMENTARY TRAINING

When you think of cross-training, you most likely think of those exercises discussed above. However, there are a number of beneficial complementary training options that also qualify as cross-training. Commonly, runners will develop their aerobic systems to a greater extent than they build their muscular system. This is an especially prevalent issue in young athletes who are still developing the strength necessary to carry their body quickly and efficiently. Often, their bodies can't support the load that they are cardiovascularly able to do and injury occurs. In other words, the engine outstrips the capabilities of the drivetrain. This issue can be mitigated by integrating cross-training in the form of weight or strength training. The obvious targets in such training are the muscle groups necessary for running fast. While it is definitely important to make those muscles stronger, it is also crucial to focus on the auxiliary muscles that support them. As the larger muscles fatigue, the support muscles come into play to a greater and greater extent. The stronger those auxiliary muscles are, the more they will be able to pick up the slack.

One of the best ways to strengthen auxiliary muscles is to incorporate drills and plyometrics into a training program. At least three times a week, athletes should be participating in skipping, jumping, bounding, lunging, and other running drills. Exercises, such as skipping with a lunge every fourth stride, that rely on balance and strength recruit muscles that aren't the main ones typically used in running. Athletes should also engage in exercises that use side-to-side and backward motion as well as forward motion. Even skipping backward can be useful in terms of using different muscles. Agility exercises will improve rhythm and coordination in running, and these types of exercises will also improve neuromuscular adaptation, which can result in better performances.

Strength training is an important form of complementary training, especially exercises targeting core, or trunk, strength. Not all injuries are caused simply by running too much. Many injuries occur because of discrepancies in leg length or because of poor biomechanics or posture. Muscular or structural weakness in an area of the body can lead to issues with running form, and cross-training can help fix these issues.

When Emily Infeld, a 10,000-meter runner, was injured leading up to the Olympic Trials in 2016, she was able to stay fit by cross-training. After sustaining a stress fracture of the left trochanter, she used the pool, the bike, and the elliptical machine in place of running. She also worked on her biomechanics and strength before going back to running. In her case, the fracture was caused by poor biomechanics, not direct impact. The limitations in mobility in her hip were causing too much friction on the bone, and eventually, the continual pulling led to a fracture. Fortunately, she worked on correcting her imbalances in time to place second at the 2016 Olympic Trials in Oregon and then eleventh at the Olympics in Rio de Janeiro, Brazil, shortly afterward.

TYPES OF CROSS-TRAINING

Now that we have sufficiently covered the benefits of cross-training, we'll discuss the different types that are most beneficial to runners. When deciding on which methods to use for supplemental training, try to choose exercises that are closest to running in terms of aerobic and muscular demands and range of motion. Many athletes find the most direct benefits result from pool running, cross-country ski machines, stationary bikes, and elliptical trainers. Because of the lower or nonexistent impact of these exercises, your athlete can safely cross-train for a longer amount of time than she would if she were running. However, most athletes use the rule of thumb of the 1:1 time ratio. For example, if you had a seven-mile run planned and that usually takes an hour, then do sixty minutes on the elliptical trainer in its place. While the time should usually remain consistent, it is safer to push yourself a little bit harder, aerobically, on the bike or elliptical than you would on a run. Experts suggest trying to maintain at least 65 percent of your heart-rate max to get the most aerobic gains.

To get a rough idea of what your target heart rate should be during aerobic exercise, you first need to estimate your maximum heart rate by using a simple calculation of 220 minus your age. From here, simply multiply the percentage of your heart rate you want to maintain to your maximum heart rate. For example, if you are eighteen years old and you want your heart rate to be 75 percent of your maximum, multiply your maximum heart rate (220 − 18 = 202) times the percentage (75 percent): 202 × .75 = 151.5.

For complementary workouts designed to focus on strength building, turn to the use of free weights, resistance bands, kettlebells, and medicine balls. When designing a strength-training program for athletes, especially runners, using both exercises that mimic the running motion and those that focus on the lesser-used support muscles is important. One of the major benefits of weight and resistance training is that these help to strengthen the typically weaker or lesser-activated muscles that, when taxed in their weaker state, fail to support proper form and lead to many running injuries. With the proper complementary exercises, however, an athlete stands a better chance of remaining healthy and strong.

9

MIND GAMES

Mantra: *Inhale love, exhale fears*

As Kevin used to emphasize to his young charges at a New Hampshire high school, races are an opportunity to experience success, not a platform for potential failure. A well-run race is exciting, a thing of inner and outer beauty and triumph. But a "bad" race is not the end of the world, even if it comes at a most inopportune time. Each challenge, be it a hard workout or a championship-level competition, is a learning experience—a chance to get more in tune with how the body and mind work together, and to learn what aspects of your preparation and execution need more work.

Running, especially racing, takes courage. Runners gather together at the start line of a race, usually in little more than a singlet, shorts, and running shoes, and give it their all, often in front of large, noisy crowds. There's no camouflage and nothing to hide behind. The time on the clock and the runner's finishing place are the only measures of success the outside world observes, yet there are often many unseen internal struggles and general hurdles runners struggle to overcome simply to get across the finish line.

While having a sharp mental edge is no substitute for good training, it can give you an advantage over the competition, and having a strong mind-body relationship can be a benefit in training, racing, and everyday life.

Mental training should be an important component of every training program. To neglect this piece of the puzzle can translate into never truly knowing how well an athlete might have performed. Not only will basic mental-skills training practices give athletes the tools they need to be successful on the track and cross-country course, but running, especially the mental aspect of it, can also teach a variety of life lessons. An athlete well-attuned to the mental aspects of his sport can learn patience, dedication, and strategy not only when running, but also when confronting the challenges of everyday life—academics, interpersonal relationships, and other common sources of self-doubt and angst. As a coach or parent, you can teach young athletes to use their minds to achieve success and also to handle perceived failure with grace and relative ease—both of which are important.

Brad suggests that high-school-age or older runners see a sports psychologist, if not regularly, at least a few times per year. Even when an athlete is experiencing success, the results can be hard to manage. He may end up putting more pressure on himself or perceiving, correctly or incorrectly, that there is more outside pressure on him—from coaches, teammates, parents, and others—to keep performing well. A psychologist can help him relax and cope with any stresses that might arise either before or after a competition or workout. A therapist might introduce the athlete to relaxation techniques, mental rehearsals, or cognitive restructuring. Cognitive restructuring helps an athlete identify disruptive thoughts that aren't accurate or productive, an important everyday coping skill for anyone but a practice that is especially useful to athletes.

Not all runners respond the same way to psychological stress or to training, so a coach needs to be aware of what each of his athletes can handle both physically and emotionally. Runners who are highly emotional might feel overwhelmed more often than others when faced with hard workouts or races. Giving everyone the exact same training plan won't produce the same results in each runner, even allowing for differences in fitness and talent. Checking in with each athlete before, during, and after workouts will help them determine how they are handling the workload. With the right coach-athlete dialogue, a runner can learn to distinguish between emotional stress and fatigue and purely physical fatigue. No matter what, yelling at or berating an athlete is not the answer. Encouragement instead of negative feedback or reinforcement is more likely to bring about positive results.

ATTITUDE MAINTENANCE

A young athlete's attitude toward both his participation in the sport and the sport itself play a major role in determining whether he achieves his goals. Sports psychology has demonstrated that attitude can affect various outcomes, from training to racing to overall health, to an even greater extent than intuition might suggest. How an athlete looks at and manages training, competition, and the outcome of an event can contribute to improved performance. The first step in improving a potentially counterproductive attitude is ensuring that everyone involved recognizes how the athlete views her current training and racing efforts and understands how a change in her attitude might affect her future goals in a positive way. Sometimes, an athlete might not realize that she is projecting a negative attitude until a dialogue is started and her awareness of her own mindset is raised; as hard as it may be to accept, most young athletes evincing negativity are not doing so owing to a conscious choice. Be willing to communicate and gently approach an athlete who is focused on the negative aspects of a given situation.

Actively fostering a positive attitude in practice can be thought of as laying the foundation for an overall positive running experience, especially during races. Runners invariably spend far more time training than they do racing. Thus practice provides a daily opportunity for athletes to rehearse engaging in the types of behaviors that will allow for the best chance of success on the track or race course.

In the same way laughter can be thought of as contagious, attitude—good or bad—can affect others, and the overall tone can spread rather quickly through a team, particularly in a daily practice setting and when the athlete with the attitude issue is a prominent member of the squad. Athletes should always be aware of the effect that their attitude can have on not only their own development but that of their teammates as well. They need to take responsibility and maintain a demeanor and presence that is beneficial to the overall emotional health and well-being of the entire team.

Physical talent and fitness are the most critical elements required for success in running, but running, like most sports, includes a tremendously mental component, and the attitude an athlete assumes during competition has a greater impact on his performance than some may realize. A runner's outlook while standing on the starting line can make the difference between a successful performance and a poor one. It's possible to be too "amped up," and it's also common to be overly blasé.

Pre-competition mental gymnastics can start minutes, hours, and even days before the event in question. Is the athlete dreading the race or the run? Is she afraid of failing? These feelings create tension and stress and build the performance into being something more than it is or should be. Coaches and parents must work with young runners to ensure they are approaching each race as an opportunity to put their training to work, not as a life-or-death or an all-or-nothing situation. This in turn requires parents and coaches to continually assure young athletes that it is not only okay to express fear or doubts, but productive and necessary. It is okay and natural for an athlete to feel nervous before a big competition, but that nervousness should take the form of excitement and anticipation rather than debilitating anxiety.

Because running places a great deal of physical stress on the body, it's important to keep overall stress to a minimum by keeping the emotional stress component as small as possible. There are many ways to do this. For example, each night, have your runner write her worries down in a journal and close the book afterward to symbolically bury those worries. This will help her sleep better, and a good night's rest will help her stay mentally focused and positive throughout the next day.

Having a plan going into a race or workout is a good way to keep your attention on the task at hand, rather than allowing it to wander or create unfavorable fantasy scenarios. Instead of allowing negative thoughts to cycle through your athlete's mind in an endless loop, encourage him to put energy into thinking about what is possible and what he can ideally achieve. The weather is something you can't change, so try not to get upset about it. Know the difference between what you can and can't change, and put your attention on the things you can change. Take note of what makes you feel comfortable before races and workouts. Decide if you are someone who prefers to warm up quietly, alone, or someone who likes to joke and chat with others so as to defuse tension. Keep your routines, but know that some flexibility in these routines is fine. Being too rigid can eventually lead to more stress.

Athletes are always pushing up against their inner demons and fears while they explore what their bodies can do. A modicum of emotional skills training should be dedicated to teaching athletes how to effectively move past such fears and trust that their bodies will respond as they have been trained to respond. It takes consistent training and racing to build the kind of self-confidence that allows an athlete to test the waters outside of her comfort zone. It helps if the athlete is focused more on the process and less on the outcome.

Though running is a tough sport that can, at times, involve some discomfort, an athlete can learn not to fear it. As a coach, don't use words like "pain" and "hurt." Focus instead on words like "taxing" or "effort." Brad notes that kids can be taught to face the fear of experiencing the discomfort associated with running hard and will ultimately learn that when they are running at an optimal level, their performance transcends their discomfort. When a runner is feeling strong and confident and is having a great race, what she might otherwise perceive as pain subjectively becomes something else, and she won't feel physical distress as intensely, if at all.

When a race or workout is going well, the challenge becomes more mental than physical: Can I push harder, even when I have fears that I won't be able to? Having a solid focus helps diminish unpleasant sensations. If an athlete is feeling uncomfortable, have him or her explain exactly where he or she feels the discomfort and describe how it feels. Focusing exquisitely on a troubling physical sensation can alter the athlete's perspective of that sensation and thereby lessen the level of perceived pain.

The last major area in which working on a positive attitude with an athlete is crucial is after a race or workout performance, regardless of the outcome. How does an athlete handle a win? How does an athlete handle a loss? How the athlete views either outcome can potentially have an effect on his mood, of course, but more importantly it can potentially influence his future performances. The way you address "successes" and "failures" and the manner in which your athlete responds play a major role in the runner's overall progress. A win or personal best should feel good and should be both acknowledged and celebrated; however, some athletes may end up wanting to rest on their laurels after a sublime effort. They may begin to think that success is, for them, a given and that it will continue to come without them having to make any changes or put forth a strong effort each time they toe the line. Good performances should serve as reinforcement that what you're doing is working, but should also be a reminder that this work needs to be continued and maybe even improved upon. This doesn't always translate into an imperative to train harder; just as often, it means continuing to train sensibly. It can sometimes be harder to stay on top than to make strides toward getting to the top.

Losses, on the other hand, are rarely fun but are inevitable in any sport. The period after a loss can be used as a time for reflection. Decide what can be improved and think of ways in which errors can be prevented in the future. Those who want to improve in their sport should use their reflections as motivation in future training sessions and competitions. However, losses should never be something runners—young or otherwise—use to determine their self-worth or overall value as a person or as an athlete. All athletes, especially youth runners, can take a bad performance very hard, so any form of punishment from parents or coaches should be categorically avoided.

GOAL SETTING

One of the most important factors in addressing the mental aspect of a training program is learning how to set goals. An athlete can't map out a plan if she doesn't know where she wants her final destination to be. At the beginning of each competitive season, have your athletes write down both their short-term and long-term goals. They should include "A-level" and "B-level" goals: "A-level" being more of a lofty goal that could feasibly happen if everything were to go as well as possible, and "B-level" being a goal that may not be an ultimate dream achievement but one that's fulfilling to the athlete nonetheless. These goals should also include both objective and subjective subgoals. For example, an objective goal may be something like "I want to qualify for the state championship" or "I want to earn my spot on the varsity team for the entire season." Tangible performance-related goals are important, serving as both direction and guidance to training behavior. However, subjective goals are just as important and crucial to the process. An example of a good subjective goal might be when an athlete states, "I want to make sure I stay engaged during the middle portion of the race where I usually tend to let my attention wander." It's also beneficial to encourage athletes to set both long-term and short-term goals. Long-term goals can include those relating to the end of the season, or they may even extend into future seasons. Short-term goals may change from race to race and should be revisited as progress is made.

Goals also serve as powerful motivators, something that every successful athlete should have. On the days that training feels unusually or inexplicably hard or an athlete begins to doubt her reasons for sticking with the sport, she can refer back to her goals and remind herself of her commitment to reaching them.

Goals also provide athletes with a sense of direction. They are a constant reminder of why the athlete is practicing every day. They also serve as reinforcement that the often grueling, physical demands of the sport are a means to an end. Each and every run, workout, and race serves as a stepping-stone taking the athlete a little bit closer to her goal. Without goals, athletes might lack the motivation to get out the door and participate. Even modest goals, such as wanting to run more miles per week, wanting to run a slightly faster time in the mile, or simply wanting to be consistent, can serve as good motivators.

VISUALIZATION

It is not uncommon for young athletes, especially those who are naturally gifted, to experience stress and anxiety from the performance-related pressure they place on themselves. To better control these stress-inducing emotions, athletes can mentally prepare for an upcoming competition by visualizing how the event will unfold beforehand. Using imagery to enhance training was popularized by the Soviets in the 1970s, when it was discovered that their Olympic athletes performed better on a regimen of visualization both before competitions and while training. This mental dress rehearsal can help create calmness in the hours and days before a race because the athlete is more likely to feel prepared to handle the task ahead in every way if he has imagined it already happening. While mental practice won't substitute for actual practice, it can greatly enhance training and is likely to help bring about positive outcomes.

There are several ways to practice visualization. One of the easiest ways is to create a running corner in your room, a place where you can put images of athletes who inspire you or anything you feel will create a positive atmosphere. Many athletes will write the time they want to run on a piece of paper and tape it to a place such as the bathroom mirror, so they see it and think about it every day. Another way to practice is to lie down in a comfortable spot. Close your eyes, and imagine yourself running the race or workout you have planned. Try to picture every step and the outcome you want, including seeing the time you wish to run on your stopwatch. Imagine how it will feel after the event. See if you can make this exercise last at least twenty minutes.

THE POWER OF MANTRAS

It's human nature to think, and humans spend most of their waking moments actively doing it. Whether consciously or subconsciously, thoughts go through your head on a consistent basis. When it comes to sports, your thoughts can either be a help or a hindrance to your performance. Endurance sports especially require a strong mind. In other sports, athletes have tangible goals or tasks, such as catching a ball or making a basket, on which to focus. When you're running, it is easy to let your mind wander, and it can be difficult to stay positive, especially when you start to experience fatigue and discomfort. Mantras are designed to direct thoughts where you want, not unlike taking control of the reins on a runaway horse.

A mantra can be any sound, word, or grouping of words said aloud or to oneself, but it should be unique and meaningful to the individual. It's actually more than simply a phrase or set of words; it's a statement that stimulates a certain emotion or feeling of calmness when it's heard or repeated. Lorraine Moller, the bronze medalist in the 1992 Olympic marathon, uses the phrase and encourages others to "run beautifully" in order to remove any adverse associations with running or the discomfort that sometimes comes with the sport. Whatever phrase an athlete decides on, it should be concise, easy to repeat, and positive. Some examples include: "I am strong and confident," "Steady and strong," "Run free," "I got this," and "I will do the best I can today."

TEN MANTRAS FOR RUNNERS

I run with confidence and strength
Comfortable and strong
I am relaxed and focused
Light and steady on my feet
I move forward with power and ease
I do my best with each challenge
No regrets
Breathe
Strong to the finish
Keep good form

To unlock the full potential of a mantra, an athlete must do more than simply choose a word or phrase. She must also repeat the phrase to herself during both stressful and stress-free times until it comes naturally to call it up during or even before times of stress. Since our thoughts can change the structure of our brains through new neural pathways, and this, in turn, can change the function of our brains—a process called neuroplasticity— repeating uplifting internal messages can eventually train the body to have a positive response. It can take time before positive thoughts and activities affect the brain, so finding and using a mantra must be practiced and perfected in order to have the most profound effect. Athletes should use their mantras during tough workouts and hard training runs. Many athletes will write the phrase down on a slip of paper and carry it with them or post it somewhere in their home as a daily reminder of what mental state they are seeking. Lucy Alexander puts these kinds of motivational quotes in her bedroom for inspiration.

POSITIVE SELF-TALK

Not too different than the mantra mentioned above is self-talk. This is the silent conversation that an athlete has with himself during a given hard effort or just in general. We can never really turn off our thoughts, but we can become aware of what kinds of dialogues are taking place in our heads. While the mantra is designed to guide thoughts and disrupt any negative self-talk, it often takes more than a simple phrase to interrupt pessimistic thoughts and encourage positivity. Learning to combat unfavorable self-talk is one of the biggest differences between champions and average athletes.

Healthy self-talk starts by first noticing what kinds of thoughts are prominent. It would be nearly impossible to think positively all the time, but learning to manage an internal dialogue can reduce stress and encourage progress in performance. An athlete should be encouraged to question the accuracy of the script that plays out in his head rather than take it as valid or fact. By participating in the dialogue, anything that is untrue, excessively harsh, or unfavorable can be countered with something more accurate and benevolent.

Part of training includes working on the mind. The best way to stay grounded, centered, and focused is to use positive "I" statements that encourage a healthy outlook about running and racing. Avoid any negative self-talk, but also avoid talking in a negative way about others. This only creates an unhealthy and uncomfortable atmosphere for everyone. Before going out to test yourself in training or a race, take two minutes to stand up tall and repeat a strong mantra or a positive phrase. This takes your attention away from the external environment and places it back on yourself, and it helps to build your confidence.

10

THE CLUB SCENE

Mantra: *I am confident*

At some point, parents need to decide whether to introduce their child to club running or running camps and, if so, how and when to do it. While most middle schools and high schools provide cross-country and track programs, these are seasonal and don't accommodate younger athletes. In most communities, you can find a number of different clubs and group running options that provide a great environment in which young athletes can experience companionship while learning the fundamentals of their sport.

From running camps to USA Track and Field (USATF) Junior Olympics programs, running clubs introduce the sports of track and field and cross-country to young runners in an enjoyable and supportive environment. For runners just starting out, most organized programs are designed to simply get kids moving and promote an active lifestyle. As the athletes mature and move into more focused training, the goal of these running clubs often shifts to helping the athletes develop specific techniques that will allow them to build strength, improve mental skills, and increase speed. This can lead to a more successful and healthier runner both in the moment and down the road.

RUNNING CAMPS

In general, when kids are given the opportunity, they like to run about and move. We humans are "designed" by evolution to move about, not sit around. We started as hunter-gatherers and the associated wiring persists in our brains. Therefore, we feel better when we're active, since at some unconscious level our physiology associates activity with literal survival.

With a bit of guidance, these kids' desire to run tends to increase. Running camps, popular during the summer months when school is out of session, are an educational and inspirational way to further a beginning or a more seasoned athlete's interest and improve his or her skill in the sport, as well as offer the opportunity to make a coterie of new friends. Usually lasting anywhere from a few days to a few weeks, these camps bring together athletes of similar ages and immerse them more fully in the sport. Most camps will divide runners into groups of similar ability, so that nobody feels overwhelmed. Not every minute of the camp is dedicated solely to running, but the primary focus, of course, is to work on becoming better athletes. In addition to running, kids will get the opportunity to meet like-minded and active people their age. The camp environment provides an opportunity for the young athletes to build lifelong friendships through the common interest of their sport while also building self-confidence.

For very young children—think elementary or middle school—it's a good idea for them to attend summer camps or other programs that cater to a number of sports and activities rather than attend camps that are limited to and focus exclusively on running and competing. It's acceptable, even good, to find a running camp, but make sure it's one that encourages balance and exposes children to a variety of activities. The main goal is to get young kids moving and active in an environment in which their individual athletic talents can emerge. For older athletes who are eager to compete in high-school cross-country and track programs, being active throughout the summer and attending a running camp can provide good base training and experience for the upcoming seasons.

Beyond providing athletes with a chance to be around other young runners, running camps allow their attendees to learn more about the sport by hosting guest speakers and providing seminars. In some of the better U.S. camps, a coach or trainer will guide athletes when it comes to running form and training schedules. Trainers, physical therapists, or massage therapists will give instructions on the best ways to stay injury-free, and they might also demonstrate the best ways to cross-train using the gym, a stationary bike, or the pool. In a camp setting, young runners will also be introduced to nutritional guidelines provided by a dietician or sports nutritionist. Often, a sports psychologist will be on hand to help athletes work on their mental skills. Bonding exercises and free time or relaxation time are a big part of most camps as well. Many young athletes can trace their love of running back to an enjoyable and positive experience at a summer camp.

SEASONAL CLUB TEAMS

Most areas in the country offer alternative running programs to school teams. While this is typically a more common option in other countries, it is becoming more common in the United States. These programs give talented young athletes the opportunity to train with coaches and teammates outside of their designated school. While this type of situation can be very beneficial for an athlete showing promise, it is one that must be navigated carefully. Club coaches have to make sure not to step on the toes of high-school or middle-school coaches. The most successful situations are ones in which the two coaches communicate and collaborate with each other, with the athletes, and with the athletes' parents. Everyone involved must understand how the runner will be training both in school programs and in club or outside groups, and mentors overseeing running groups outside of school programs need to help the athlete arrive to his or her next season fit and excited to run, not overworked.

The Land Sharks Running Club, a youth running club based in Colorado, is a five-week-long program offered to kids between the ages of five and eighteen in the spring and the fall. The elementary-school group consists of kids in kindergarten through fifth grade. According to Bean Wrenn, one of the parents and coaches assisting in the Boulder, Colorado, area, the club is focused on introducing running to kids at a young age but in a noncompetitive environment. Practices are focused less on structured running and more on introducing running in the form of games and group activities. Wrenn notes that sometimes the kids don't even realize they are running because they are so focused on the games they play. For example, on a hot day, Wrenn might suggest that the kids participate in a water relay, a game in which she lines up two buckets across the field. The kids then have to run back and forth, take water out of one bucket using a Dixie cup, and run it across the field to fill up the empty bucket. Coaches split the kids into two teams, and the goal is to see which team fills the empty bucket first. The kids dedicate their attention to the task at hand and therefore don't always realize how much continuous activity they are getting, especially when parents, siblings, and spectators are cheering them on. When the children are having fun, feeling supported, and feeling like they are part of the group or community, they are more likely to come back for more. More importantly, they are more likely to include running as a lifelong activity.

Wrenn's own children participated in Land Sharks and Melody Fairchild's Mountain Warriors kids group when they were younger. They were also a part of the Boulder Track Club's (BTC) track night for kids, a program that coincided with a twice-a-month summer series of track races open to the public, and her daughter enrolled in a separate preparatory program offered in the spring that's designed to help kids get ready for the Bolder Boulder 10K road race, one of the largest races in the country. Many kids participate in Fleet Feet's running program for kids, which takes place in the spring and the fall over the course of six weeks at various elementary schools in Colorado. Children between the ages of six and ten can join the Mountain Lions team. Twice a week, up to fifteen kids meet with a coach and volunteer assistant coaches to run and engage in activities such as stretching, drills, and games to improve running form and performance. There are at least two optional races offered during each six-week session.

The Bolder Boulder training club in which Wrenn's daughter, Marist, participated is one of several offered to both children and adults in the Boulder area. Leading up to the race, participants meet once a week on Sundays to warm up, run a few miles, and engage in specific drills with former Olympic marathon runner Colleen De Reuck. Even after skipping a few sessions, Marist, who was eight years old at the time, was able to run an impressive 51:26 for the 10K race. Wrenn attributes her daughter's endurance to playing soccer and being generally active from the time she was young, but there's no doubt that the running programs helped her become a faster, more focused runner.

For Lucy Alexander, joining a running club was what helped her realize how much she loved athletics. When Lucy's mother, Neirda, dragged her reluctant daughter to her first Little Athletics session, she suspected Lucy might enjoy herself, but she didn't anticipate the extent to which this would prove true. Immediately after the memorable session, Lucy, smiling and excited, ran over to her mother and asked if they could go buy a pair of spikes. She was sold and kept going to the summer sessions so she could learn each event, from sprints to distance running. Lucy eventually found out that she excels in distance events.

During her second season with Little Athletics, Lucy met John Bowers, an older gentleman who coaches primarily younger distance runners three times a week in Australia. He also supports his athletes by attending their school, regional, and national races. Lucy decided to join his group and has been enjoying it ever since. Bowers and his wife feel that it's important to provide a fun and social atmosphere for the kids in his program and their parents. Bowers's wife will even provide tea and coffee for the parents who come out to attend sessions with their children, and once a month everyone gets to indulge in cake to celebrate the kids who happen to have a birthday that month. And he does this all for free, so great is his love for the sport. It's people like Bowers who provide great experiences that will ultimately encourage kids to stay active throughout their lives.

One of the most successful national running programs in the United States is Girls on the Run, a nonprofit organization geared toward helping young girls form healthy relationships with their bodies, their peers, and their communities. The ten-week after-school program inspires girls to be the best version of themselves they can be by allowing them to set goals and participate in running events and noncompetitive races. There are two age groups available to young girls: third through fifth grade, and sixth through eighth grade; the affiliated Heart and Sole program provides guidance to adolescent girls. In addition to learning about themselves and their peers, the girls are encouraged to give back to their communities by organizing and taking part in charitable activities. Through physical fitness, the Girls on the Run club teaches healthy habits that encourage lifelong fitness and a positive lifestyle.

For a more organized and consistent training environment, there are seasonal club teams with varying levels of seriousness and competitiveness. The Junior Olympics program, a USA Track and Field (USATF) organization that has been around since the mid-1960s, is a great option for athletes wanting to incorporate significant competitions into their summer training. The program provides opportunities for children to compete in six age groups: 8 and under, 9–10, 11–12, 13–14, 15–16, and 17–18. According to the USATF website (www.USATF.org), the Junior Olympics program is one of the most popular youth development programs in the country, with as many as seventy thousand children participating each year; many former participants have gone on to qualify for the Olympic Games. The program offers a series of competitions in preliminary, association, and regional meets, culminating in the National Championships in either track and field or cross-country.

While clubs and camps can be a great way to introduce young kids to running or allow them to become more focused, parents need to be aware of areas in which the coach might be lacking. Ideally, a coach will address nutrition, emotional health, recovery, and training, but sometimes one or more of these topics will slip through the cracks, leaving the job to parents or to the athlete himself. A main concern when placing kids into a running program is making sure they maintain balance in their lives. Running too much year-round can lead to injuries and burnout, so make sure any club or camp coaches know not only what each child will be running but also how he will be training throughout the year. A coach needs to know when the child will be racing and what his training will look like leading up to those races, but she also needs to know when the athlete will be resting or taking time off from running. Everyone needs to be on the same page, so that the athlete doesn't get into a pattern of running or competing too much year-round.

11

DECISIONS

Mantra: *Progress, not perfection*

Once an athlete has made the choice to start running, there are still important decisions to be made. While it isn't necessary for a young runner to specialize in one event early on, she must consider both what events she likes and also where her talents shine most brightly. If you take a glimpse of any track and field team, you will see athletes of many shapes and sizes. While all of them may enjoy the same sport, there's a big difference in the skill set of a high jumper versus that of a thrower or a distance runner. Unless an athlete expresses interest in participating in a discipline that includes multiple events, such as the decathlon, eventually focusing on one type of training will allow an athlete to reach her goals more quickly and thoroughly.

There isn't a "one size fits all" way to train for success. If an athlete makes the decision to participate in longer distances, she and her coach must determine the best way to go about training based on her unique qualities as a runner. Age, development, and injury history all play a role in how an athlete responds to a given regimen and must be considered when a coach is designing a specific training program.

As an example, two runners who both want to race the mile may end up benefiting from two very different training schedules. One may thrive on low mileage with a lot of plyometrics and strength training, while the other may benefit from higher mileage and lower-intensity activities. Both may end up running well in that event despite the very different approaches.

The job of a coach is to determine the best way for an athlete to succeed while remaining happy and healthy.

EVENT SPECIALIZATION

The longer an athlete remains in the sport, the more likely it is that he will begin to show promise in a specific event. Early on, however, it is important for athletes to try a variety of distances and events. Not only will they benefit from the various demands of each competition, but they will also open themselves up to finding their true potential, possibly in events they hadn't considered previously. Young athletes should be encouraged to try everything from sprints to distance races and should be supported even if they choose to try field events.

When athletes develop and mature, it's likely that their individual qualities will draw them toward specializing in one area. The coach should play an integral role in this decision without forcing it. It's important for the athlete to feel passionate about competing in the event he chooses, so the coach should listen to his athlete's input. Brad notes that motivation plays a big role in getting an athlete to run well. If the athlete likes the event, he is more likely to want to train well for it. Expose athletes to a variety of distances to find their natural talents, but also listen to the athletes to help determine what events they enjoy doing. An athlete can move up in distance or even down if it suits him, but, in most cases, it's easier for an athlete to move up in distance as he matures.

STRENGTH VS. SPEED

While talent and ability can certainly be developed, the majority of young athletes will show more potential in either the longer events or the shorter events, although in exceptional cases, athletes crop up who are gifted at both. This is determined predominantly by where they fall on the spectrum of endurance versus speed. While both of these qualities can be cultivated and developed, most runners show a natural tendency toward one or the other. This is a function of basic physiology.

Muscle make-up in humans includes a genetically determined blend of slow-twitch (Type I) and fast-twitch (Type II) muscle fibers. The proportion of one versus the other plays a big role in which events an athlete is more likely to be successful. A biopsy can determine the exact percentage that an athlete has, but most coaches should have a pretty good idea of where an athlete falls on the spectrum of fast-twitch and slow-twitch fibers based on their training and overall ability. Sprinters in events 400 meters and below usually have at least 50 percent fast-twitch fibers. Middle-distance runners specializing in the 800 meters or 1,500 meters tend to have between 35 percent and 40 percent fast-twitch fibers. Pure distance athletes who are better suited for the 5,000 meters and up usually have up to 85 percent slow-twitch fibers. If an athlete simply can't get her legs to turn over quickly but can pound out lap after lap on the track without slowing, chances are her muscles are made up of more slow-twitch fibers than fast-twitch.

While an athlete may show early on that she has the qualities necessary to become a great distance runner, strength training is an essential accessory that needs to be added to her training program slowly and conservatively. Basic endurance is developed mainly by integrating training that includes long runs and threshold work. Young athletes aren't always able to handle these types of training components, but initially, volume should always take precedence over intensity. A young athlete will naturally improve her performance by simply doing comparatively easy training runs for a period of eight to twelve weeks. Quality speed training is something that should be incorporated only after strength and endurance has been achieved. A runner's tissues, muscles, and auxiliary muscles must be developed enough to handle high-intensity running.

For very young runners, running somewhat faster for very short distances is fine, as long as the training is done on soft surfaces as much as possible and the intensity isn't extreme. Short bursts of speed when they play a game of tag is a good example. This type of running may serve as both speed and endurance training to younger athletes. There's no need to push a youngster to run a lot of steady mileage.

Regardless of the type of athlete, young runners should be encouraged to do strides—bursts of about twenty seconds at close to all-out sprinting pace—speed development drills, and, when more developed, actual speed work. These types of activities will help create a better overall athlete.

WHEN AND WHERE TO RACE

As a coach of young runners, one of the most important decisions you must make is when, where, and how often your athletes should race. This decision is usually made easier by determining the goals of each athlete and the best ways to achieve them. Some athletes, especially those new to the sport, may lack racing experience. Within reason, such athletes can benefit greatly from running in low-key meets or noncompetitive time trials more frequently than others, simply to gain experience. Each race provides an opportunity for the athlete to learn something new about the sport and that particular event, and keeping competitions relatively close together provides a chance to put those lessons to the test while they are still fresh in her mind. Runners who are more experienced and may already be specializing in an event may be more suited to pick out important competitions during the season to target. More developed and experienced athletes are also more likely to be able to push closer to their full potential in races, meaning that they require more recovery time between each competition.

In addition to knowing how often athletes should race, it is also essential for a coach to know which races should be a given competitor's main focus. Again, every athlete is different, and there isn't a single best approach that applies to everyone. In some situations, an athlete can benefit greatly from taking part in a low-key race in which the chance of a higher placement is likely. This way, there's a good chance that he can gain a boost in confidence if he runs up to his potential. A coach must know both how her own runners and how other runners typically perform in order to make this kind of decision. Other athletes tend to perform better in high-pressure situations or championship races where there will be many good runners against whom to race. Using feedback from the athlete, it is up to the coach to make a judgment call on which approach will be most productive.

Except for those competing in the shorter distances, it is fairly uncommon for collegiate and professional athletes to run more than one event in a one-day track meet. However, if you attend a high-school track meet, you are likely to see faster athletes—who can often afford to go less than all-out and win anyway—running up to two or more events. Letting athletes compete in several different races in a meet can give them the opportunity to try their hand at racing various distances as opposed to merely training for them. With a limited number of meets each season, running multiple distances provides more than one chance to try different races and see what works out best.

⑫

THROUGH THE AGES

Mantra: *I am fearless*

Running is often regarded, perhaps rightfully so, as the "purest" of sports. It requires a minimum of equipment and thus finances, and you don't need to be able to field or hit softballs, throw or catch footballs, or learn a pick-and-roll or what a zone defense means. You don't need a ski pass or to pay golf greens fees. And you're certainly unlikely to be cross-checked into the boards at Madison Square Garden by a half-crazed defenseman on skates.

This, however, leads to a lot of confusion. Yes, running, is "merely" putting one foot in front of the other. This in turn engenders the understandable but erroneous conclusion that because pretty much anyone can take up running, its subtleties and nuances can be effectively disregarded. In the past, people might have believed that you either run fast or you don't, and if you don't, you will never get your time in the spotlight. Here's your participation ribbon or maybe even your varsity letter, but set aside any hope of making a career out of it. Today, things are different, with companies offering products and other types of compensation to athletes of all ages and abilities. There are opportunities for trust funds and sponsorships that weren't available even in the early 1980s.

Knowledge concerning training, recovery, and mental skills in running keeps evolving. It wasn't all that long ago that women were banned from racing anything longer than the 800 meters on the track. The 1984 Olympics, in fact, while well-known for hosting the first Olympic women's marathon, were the first Games in which there were any events for women longer than 1,500 meters. The female pioneers in the sport eventually fought for the right to participate in longer races and demonstrated that not only can women run long distances; they can run them fast. After super-famous talk-show hostess Oprah Winfrey—who had candidly struggled with her weight for her whole adult life—completed the Marine Corps marathon in 1994, people all over the globe started to believe that they too could "just do it," and a running boom was born.

But this wasn't the first such "boom." Starting in the 1970s, shortly after Frank Shorter won the gold medal in the 1972 Olympic marathon, running became more popular, especially in the United States. Today, you see more and more people running road races, marathons, mountain races, and even ultramarathons. The key to running later in life, however, isn't to do as much as humanly possible early on; it's more to create a system of training and racing that's healthy, sensible, and enjoyable. As long as an athlete is choosing a reasonable training plan and keeping physically and emotionally healthy, the chances of her continuing to run later in life are high.

When working with very young children, the main goal of a running program should be teaching them to enjoy being active. Helping kids make exercise a habit will encourage them to continue being active into adulthood and even into old age. As humans age, it can become more difficult to continue running. This is something children might not understand. When kids are active, they might feel indestructible. Once past the age of thirty-five, though, both VO2 Max and muscle mass begin to decline. In addition, general wear and tear on the body can lead to stiffening joints, limited flexibility, and poor coordination. After the age of sixty, these limitations increase at an even more extreme rate. To some extent, the "use it or lose it" motto becomes a reality the older an athlete gets, but the key is to use "it" the right amount. Proper stretching, adjustments to training, and cross-training can help ease an athlete from one age group to the next.

STRETCHING

Quadriceps

This stretch is done standing upright. Your athlete can use her free hand on a chair if she feels unstable. Instruct her to pull her right leg behind her using her left hand. As much as possible, have her keep her knee pointing straight downward. She should hold the stretch for ten seconds and then push the top of her foot into her hand for another ten seconds. This will engage the opposite muscle. Have her go back to the original stretch for a few seconds more before switching legs.

Groin

Have your athlete start by sitting in a comfortable position with his legs crossed, like one would when asked to sit cross-legged on the floor at school. To stretch the groin, your athlete will bring the bottoms of her feet together and allow her knees to fall toward the floor. If this is easy for her, have her use her hands to press her knees toward the floor.

Piriformis

Instruct your athlete to lie on his back with his left foot flat on the floor and his left knee bent. His right leg should be straight out. Make sure his back is as flat as he can make it on the floor. He should make sure not to arch his lower back. Have him pull his left knee up toward his chest. Using his right hand, instruct him to grab his left knee and pull it toward his right (opposite) shoulder. He should hold the stretch for at least twelve seconds. Repeat on the right side.

Psoas

This stretch starts in a lunge position with one leg out in front of the other. The first step is to have your athlete tuck her tailbone underneath her as much as possible. She should feel a stretch along the front of her thigh. From this position, tell her to lean forward, stretching the front of the leg even more.

Hamstrings

If your athlete is doing stretches alone and doesn't have a partner to help him with a facilitated hamstring stretch, simply instruct him to sit on the ground with one foot out in front of him and the other bent with the bottom of his foot lightly resting against the inner thigh of the opposite leg. His knee will fall toward the ground on the bent leg. Tell him to lean forward with his back straight and his head aiming toward the knee of his outstretched leg. He can then rotate the leg both inward and outward to see the difference in what part of the hamstring is stretched. (Note: for very tight hamstrings, stretching and working on the feet can be helpful in releasing tight hamstring muscles.)

Arms

Start by having your athlete stand with her feet hip-width apart, keeping her knees slightly bent. Instruct her to raise her left arm up straight by her ear. From this position, she will bend her arm at the elbow, dropping her left hand toward her right shoulder behind her back. She should feel a stretch on the underside of her arm. From this point, have her point her fingers down to touch the back of her shoulder blade. For a deeper stretch, she can gently pull her left elbow toward her head with her right hand until she feels the stretch. Have her hold the stretch about thirty seconds for each arm.

Back

This is a gentle stretch that's good for the back. Start by having your athlete kneel on all fours with his hands squarely beneath his shoulders and his knees below his hips. Instruct him to tighten his core muscles as he exhales and arches his spine. You can tell him to think of a swayback pony. Make sure he keeps his core muscles tight as he changes position and rounds his back, like a scared cat on Halloween. Have him transition slowly between the two movements, and make sure he holds each peak position for about ten seconds.

Calves

Instruct your athlete to face a wall with her legs even and her feet below her hips. Have her move her right leg forward, so that her toe is close to the wall, and then she can extend her left leg straight back, placing her heel flat on the floor. Tell her to try to keep her back knee straight. Have her lean toward the wall until she feels the stretch in the calf of her straightened leg. She should hold the stretch for thirty seconds and then raise herself up on the toes of her straightened leg for a few seconds. When she moves back into the stretch, she should be able to stretch the area more deeply. Have her hold the position again for twenty seconds before switching sides.

Glutes

Instruct your athlete to sit on the floor with his left leg straight in front of him and his right leg straight, not twisted, but with his knee bent. Have him gently twist his torso toward the right side or his bent knee until he feels a stretch in his buttocks. He should hold the stretch for thirty seconds. For a deeper stretch, he can sit in the same position but bend his right knee over the left leg, so his foot is resting near the inner side of his left leg. Repeat the stretch on the opposite side.

Sides

This is a standing stretch. Use a chair for balance if needed. Have your athlete stand with her feet directly under her hips and her legs straight but her knees very slightly bent, just so that they are not locked. Instruct her to place her right leg behind her left. Both feet should be on the floor with the left flat on the ground and the right with the outer edge resting on the floor. Have her push her right hip out to the side until she feels the stretch in her hip and side. She may also feel a stretch on the outside of the thigh. Have her hold for thirty seconds. Repeat three times on each side.

OLDER RUNNERS

There are many examples of outstanding performances of older runners. For example, Hal Higdon, a four-time World Masters Championships winner in the 3,000-meter steeplechase during the 1970s and early 1980s, ran a remarkable 2:29 marathon at the age of fifty-two, and in 2014, Christine Kennedy ran an outstanding 2:59 marathon at the age of fifty-nine. Kennedy was also the winner of the 2011 World Masters Track and Field Championships in the 5,000, where she ran 19:36 in extremely hot conditions. Though these kinds of extraordinary times are not the norm once a runner passes the age of forty or so, there are plenty of older runners who participate in races that range in distance from sprints to ultramarathons.

One of the biggest factors in being able to run later in life is learning self-care and learning to read what your body needs. Remaining healthy throughout life means making necessary adjustments to training programs, to diet, and to recovery times as the body changes. Looking at the long-term goals of running is prudent, but it's the focus on more immediate rewards that motivate most people to stay active. When an athlete knows that going on a run will reduce stress and help improve mood, it's easier for her to lace up her shoes and get out the door. It's important for coaches to understand that healthy, long-lasting habits can be taught at a young age.

In order to make exercise fun, coaches like Barb Higgins of New Hampshire keep overly structured training out of the picture until high school, focusing instead on games such as scavenger hunts that keep the kids fit and moving without putting them in a disciplined training situation. She teaches drills and the fundamentals of running in a way that's enjoyable for the children. Bean Wrenn, one of the coaches in the Land Sharks program in Colorado and a mother of three, stresses that kids do well and want to continue participating if the environment is noncompetitive and the overall running mileage is kept to a minimum. The kids enjoy the games the coaches organize for them. Games include water relays on hot days, team relays in which the kids must work together, and other activities, including some running. When races are held, the distances are no longer than two miles, and the focus is on participation, not winning. During the off-season, instead of following a running-specific training program, kids are encouraged to participate in other sports, such as soccer, swimming, gymnastics, or basketball.

ADDITIONAL DRILLS AND DYNAMIC STRETCHING

Most drills should be done in one or two sets of about ten to fifteen repetitions that translates to a distance of about twenty meters.

Ankling

This is a running drill with quick, short steps. Keeping the stride very short, almost nonexistent, have your athlete engage his glutes and take quick steps forward focusing on pushing the foot down, landing on the forefoot. Just as his foot rolls down, before the heel completely touches flat on the ground, he should push off to a new stride. The steps should be small but purposeful with minimal knee lift. The idea is for the athlete to move quickly. Make sure his arms are also moving in sync with the quick pace of his legs.

Ankle Springs

Your athlete should use a short, bouncy stride without pushing down with her foot as she jogs forward while leaning forward as she progresses. Her foot should come through while she holds a neutral foot stance with her knees partly extended and locked. Tell her to think of her ankle being like a spring. She should use the momentum to keep propelling herself forward. Her focus should be on taking steps with her feet striking the ground directly underneath her.

Arm Pullbacks

While he is walking, instruct your athlete to keep his shoulders level and straight while he leans slightly forward. With his arms held at 90 degrees bent at the elbows, he can imagine trying to touch his elbows behind him by contracting the muscles in his back to pull his chest out and his arms closer together in back of him. He should feel the muscles between his shoulder blades contract.

D-Skips

Have your athlete skip with high knees, but as he raises the knee up toward the sky, he should bring it up at a 45-degree angle to the outside.

Backward Skipping

This is harder than it sounds at first. Once your athlete gets the hang of it, though, she might find it a pleasant exercise. Be sure to warn your athlete to occasionally look behind her, so she doesn't trip over anything. Using the same form she uses in regular skipping, instruct your athlete to skip backward. Her lean should be very gently backward instead of forward on this drill.

Walking or Skipping Lunge

Have your athlete start by simply walking or skipping. Make sure she maintains a tall, erect posture that will help prevent her knees from going over her toes while in the lunge position. As she begins to step forward with her left leg, make sure she is stable and carefully drops to a lunge position. She will lower herself down, keeping her hips square, until her right knee almost touches the ground. Coming up out of the position, instruct her to drive her right heel into the ground and push herself back up and into the next step forward. Repeat with the opposite leg.

Kickouts

For this drill, instruct your athlete to keep both knees slightly flexed at full extension while he moves forward walking and lifts one leg high into the air. He should come up on the toes of his supporting leg. As the extended leg comes forward, he should crunch forward leaning his chest toward his thigh as he reaches the opposite arm toward the extended leg. The other arm should naturally swing back to counterbalance the motion.

Bounds

Bounding is an exaggerated and powerful stride. When done correctly, the athlete looks like a gazelle, suspended in the air for much longer than when a normal running stride is taken. Have your athlete begin by jogging, and when he's ready, he will push off his supporting foot as usual but with a lot more force, so that he is propelled into the air as he brings the knee of the lead leg up higher than normal. His opposite arm should be in synch with the exaggerated motion, raised up high to match the high position of leading leg. Upon landing, he will immediately push off in the same dynamic fashion with the opposite foot.

Walking Toe Raisers

Instruct your athlete to begin walking forward. When ready, have her rise up on her toes as she propels herself forward with each step. Think of a slightly exaggerated walk or high knees without actually bringing the knees up high. Make sure she keeps good upper body running posture and arm motion with this drill.

Strides

Encourage your athlete to use strides to warm up before races or workouts. The strides should be approximately 50 to 60 meters in length. Instruct your athlete to begin slowly and gradually pick up his running pace until he briefly reaches a speed that's close to race pace. Quickly scale the pace back down to a jog before stopping.

Leg Swings

Instruct your athlete to stand facing a wall, a chair, a fence, or a pole for support. With your athlete standing on one leg while holding the wall for support, have her swing one leg up to about hip level back and forth in front of her, pivoting on her standing leg as she does. Make sure she keeps her legs straight without locking her knee.

TRAINING YOUNG RUNNERS

Controversy invariably arises when it comes to the topic of training young runners to compete. How much mileage can they do and still remain healthy? How much speed work should they tackle? Should they race year-round? There are many aspects of a young runner's life to consider when creating a training plan. Opinions will vary, of course, but there are some indisputable guidelines to follow that will likely lead to a more successful and healthy runner. Too often, coaches and mentors don't think about how the running someone does at a young age will affect her down the road. It's a good idea to look at the ways in which a coach can most effectively deliver his athletes to the running program one level up the chain (e.g., junior high to high school, high school to college). This includes making sure that they haven't been physically and mentally tapped before reaching high school or college, yet have assembled a broad fitness base and had the experience of racing intensely and well. Adding a dose of fun is essential for staving off boredom and keeping runners relaxed. Incorporating games and guiding kids in a given direction rather than forcing them to take those paths are good ways to encourage runners to stay in it over the long haul. Designing enjoyable running programs for children in grade school when there is no structured competition is less challenging than creating fun programs for older kids. Once runners are in high school, it's more difficult to keep the pressure off and the training sensible.

When it comes to high-school runners, one of the difficulties in designing a training schedule is the constraints imposed by the interscholastic schedule. With the team's obligation to participate in certain races throughout the season, there's little room for variation. Races are usually held every Saturday during both the cross-country and track seasons, with other meets on given weekdays. This often means that the entire team must be on a weekly "microcycle" (a short, distinct training period) and the same "mesocycle" (a series of microcycles that may be repeated in a single season) even if some of those runners might need longer rest phases during their training or develop aerobic conditioning at different rates. For example, if a runner does better on a ten-day training cycle, chances are he won't race as well if he does a hard workout early in the week and then has to race on Saturday before he is fully recovered. For those who can recover more quickly, a seven-day cycle of training isn't a problem. Having to train an entire group of kids makes it nearly impossible to individualize runners' training. This means that for some kids, the training will be either inappropriately hard or too easy; only for a select few will it be optimal.

Bobby McGee, author of *Magical Running* and other books and the coach of numerous world-class runners and triathletes, has this to say on the subject: "Frequency teaches skill and long periods teach fitness, but how these are introduced depends on the mental and emotional maturity of an individual." Too often, coaches think that they can broadly apply all principles of training, but the best programs are the ones in which each member of the team is seen as an individual.

The greater the extent to which a coach can create individualized training programs, the better off the team will be. It is essential to "type" each runner in order to develop an appropriate running schedule. Because some kids can be extremely competitive, coaches must be careful to keep teammates from racing each other during workouts so that the competitive edge isn't exhausted during training (this phenomenon of "leaving races on the practice course" is distressingly common among kids). For example, splitting the team into smaller groups for workouts or having kids start their intervals thirty seconds apart will keep unnecessary rivalries to a minimum. Running at its core is an individual sport, but cross-country is a group endeavor in which individuals draw inspiration from each other because of the commonality of purpose, so everyone benefits from the support of the team as long as teammates don't become nemeses.

An optimal summer and early-season training plan for a high-school runner can include running in excess of seventy miles per week, but most teens won't be able to handle that kind of mileage, and many of those who could handle the workload might not be interested in running that much. The good news is that most kids don't have to run extraordinarily high mileage in order to achieve success in cross-country or on the track. Plenty of distance runners have enjoyed success on as little as thirty miles a week, with some even winning state titles in cross-country on such a regimen; understand that these runners are also outliers. The "sweet spot" for most kids lies somewhere in between. How those miles are allocated is vitally important. To a point, the more miles a runner can bank, the more fitness and stamina she will build, but mileage has to remain within a runner's physical, emotional, and mental capabilities.

Ultimately, good training doesn't end up being entirely about weekly mileage, though consistency is important. Determining how many miles per week a young athlete should run depends on her history in the sport, her overall health, and how she responds to gradual increases in mileage. Some coaches do away with mileage and opt for training by minutes or a combination of recording miles and minutes instead. This can help reduce the desire to add miles simply for the sake of adding miles and keep the focus on quality training instead. Remember, the goal is to run well, not simply to run a lot of miles.

Without the aid of banned drugs, such as erythropoietin (EPO), a protein hormone that helps stimulate the production of red blood cells, and other performance-enhancing techniques, coaches must pay attention to recovery and how much training their athletes can handle without risking injury and excessive fatigue. Great athletes are produced when a coach can determine the right training combined with good nutrition and the proper amount of rest for each of his athletes, but a coach's role is more than turning out capable athletes. A coach is a guide, someone who encourages his athletes on their road to self-discovery, and on this path is where each reaches for her destiny and finds all that she can accomplish.

CONCLUSION

Ensuring that young athletes who are successful remain so as they mature into adulthood is a primary theme of this book and is woven throughout its chapters. One of the best examples of someone who was able to have tremendous success as a young athlete and carry her accomplishments into adulthood is Melody Fairchild, the standout runner from Boulder, Colorado. As a high-school runner and eight-time state champion, Fairchild became the first girl in the United States to run under ten minutes for two miles. She ran an incredible 9:55—indoors, at that. Additionally, she won the Foot Locker Cross-Country Championships twice and set the course record—which still stands as of this writing—by running the 5K at Balboa Park in San Diego in 16:39. At the 1991 Junior World Cross-Country Championships in Antwerp, Belgium, Fairchild took the bronze medal.

Fairchild's accomplishments continued throughout her college career in Oregon, where she was an NCAA all-American in track and cross-country. In 1996, she won the NCAA 3,000-meter indoor race and also qualified for the Olympic Trials in the 10K. She later qualified for the Olympic marathon trials, but these incredible feats and more were just the beginning.

As a masters runner, Fairchild has continued to set course records, win, and place in the top ten in mountain and road races around the globe. Despite her palette of excellence, she often flies under the radar and doesn't outright seek the spotlight. Her accomplishments speak for themselves, but she hasn't stopped at incredible athletic achievements. Fairchild has also stepped into the role of coach, mentor, and even mother. She is seen by many as one of the most well-rounded, accomplished, down-to-earth individuals in the sport. Her endless smile and the twinkle in her eye give the impression that she truly loves not just what she's doing, but also giving back. She makes running part of her social agenda, sharing and interacting with others to make the sport more enjoyable for everyone involved. Through all her triumphs and spectacular efforts, she somehow managed to find balance, and this is essential when it comes to longevity in the sport.

Following an example that someone like Fairchild sets shows how a successful training program that focuses on self-discovery, health, and balance can keep young runners happy and healthy while maximizing their chances for a long, successful competitive career as adults.

BIBLIOGRAPHY

Alexander, Lucy. Personal interview. 7 July 2016.

Alexander, Nerida. Personal interview. 7 July 2016.

The American College of Sports Medicine. "The Female Athlete Triad." http://www.acsm.org/docs/brochures/the-female-athlete-triad.pdf.

Beck, Kevin. "The Thin Men." *Running Times Magazine*, April 2000. http://www.runnersworld.com/health/thin-men.

Brittin, Elizabeth. "Training on Empty." Smashwords. 2012.

Fairchild, Melody. Personal interview. 6 Feb. 2014.

Fry, Scott. Personal interview. 22 April 2012.

Hansen, Dr. Richard. Personal interview. 11 July 2016.

Harvard Medical School/Helpguide.org. "Vitamins & Minerals." http://www.helpguide.org/harvard/vitamins-and-minerals.htm.

Higgins, Barb. Personal interview. 14 April 2014.

McGee, Bobby. Personal interview. 13 March 2013.

McGettigan-Dumas, Róisín. Personal interview. 20 Aug. 2016.

Moller, Lorraine. Personal interview. 21 May 2011.

Plaatjes, Mark. Personal interview. 12 March 2014.

Scott, Paul. "When Being Varsity-Fit Masks an Eating Disorder." The *New York Times*, September 14, 2006. http://www.nytimes.com/2006/09/14/fashion/14Fitness.html.

Strout, Erin. "How Emily Infeld Cross-Trained Her Way To The Olympics." *Runner's World*, July 7, 2016. http://www.runnersworld.com/olympic-trials/how-emily-infeld-cross-trained-her-way-to-the-olympics.

Walker, Rebecca. Personal interview. 19 April 2016.
Waller, Ruth. Personal interview. 24 Aug. 2016.
Weich, Greg. Personal interview. 27 March 2016.
Wrenn, Bean. Personal interview. 19 Nov. 2012.

SUGGESTED RESOURCES

ACTIVITIES AND SPORTS FOR KIDS

JumpBunch: kids fitness games, fun sports activities.
  jumpbunch.com/kids-click-here/fitness-games/.
Kid Activities (Barb Shelby): outdoor games for school-age kids.
  www.kidactivities.net/category/Games-Outside-Play.aspx.
Kids & Sports: book on physical activity and kids' health.
    Small, Eric, and Sheryl Swoopes. *Kids & Sports: Everything You and Your Child Need to Know About Sports, Physical Activity, and Good Health—A Doctor's Guide for Parents and Coaches.* New York: Newmarket Press, 2009.

EATING DISORDER INFORMATION

ANRED: anorexia and eating disorders information and resources.
  www.anred.com/.
ED Referral Service: top rated for anorexia, bulimia, binge eating help. The world's most comprehensive treatment finding service.
  edreferral.com/.
MentalHelp.net: website providing mental health and mental illness information, including for eating disorders.
  www.mentalhelp.net/articles/eating-disorders/.
NEDA: National Eating Disorders Association.
  www.nationaleatingdisorders.org/.

INDIVIDUALS, COACHES, AND GROUP RESOURCES

Bobby McGee: Olympic coach, author, and speaker.
  www.bobbymcgee.com/.
  McGee, Bobby. *Magical Running*. Boulder, CO: Bobbysez Publishing, 2000.
Lorraine Moller: author, coach, and bronze medalist in the Olympic marathon.
  Moller, Lorraine. *On the Wings of Mercury*. Dunedin, New Zealand: Longacre
    Press, 2007.
Melody Fairchild: athlete, coach, and speaker.
  melodyfairchild.com/.

JOURNALS

Burfoot, A. *Runner's World Training Journal: A Daily Dose of Motivation, Training
  Tips and Running Wisdom for Every Kind of Runner—From Fitness Joggers to
  Competitive Racers*. New York: Rodale, 2006.
Chronicle Books Staff. *Runner's Journal: A Year of Running*. San Francisco, CA:
  Chronicle Books, 2013.
The Kid's Running Journal! Getting Started on the Right Foot. Smarter Journals
  and Notebooks, 2016.

NUTRITION FOR ATHLETES

Clark, N. *Nancy Clark's Food Guide for New Runners: Getting It Right the First
  Time*. Maidenhead, UK: Meyer & Meyer Sport, 2009.
———. *Nancy Clark's Sports Nutrition Guidebook*. Champaign, IL: Human Kinet-
  ics, 1997.

PHYSICAL THERAPY AND THERAPISTS

Boulder Center for Sports Medicine.
  www.bouldersportsmedicine.org/.
Dr. Richard Hansen, D.C.: High Altitude Spine & Sport.
  highaltitudesportsrehab.com/.
Marcus Hille, physical therapist.
  marcusallenhille.com/.

PHYSIOLOGY, SCIENCE, AND HEALTH

Healthy Kids Running Series: provides a healthy kids running program.
www.healthykidsrunningseries.org/.
KidsHealth: the Web's most visited site about children's health.
kidshealth.org/.
Tween and Teen Health: useful website article on strength training for kids.
Mayo Clinic Staff. "Tween and Teen Health." www.mayoclinic.org/healthy-life
style/tween-and-teen-health/in-depth/strength-training/art-20047758.
Textbook of Running Medicine: information on injuries and health.
O'Connor, Francis G., Robert P. Wilder, and Robert Nirschl. *Textbook of Run-
ning Medicine*. New York: McGraw-Hill, Medical Division, 2001.
The Science of Running: book on running and training.
Magness, Steve. *The Science of Running: How to Find Your Limit and Train to
Maximize Your Performance*. San Rafael, CA: Origin Press, 2014.

RUNNING CAMPS

Team Prep USA: high-elevation training, running camps, coaching, advanced teen
camp.
www.teamprepusarunning.com/.
RunningCamps.org: America's Guide for Running Camps and Clinics: useful re-
source to find a running camp.
camps.milesplit.com/find.
Mountain Warriors Program: multiple running programs with Melody Fairchild.
melodyfairchild.com/program-registration/.

RUNNING CLUBS AND GROUPS

Girls on the Run: nonprofit girls' empowerment program.
www.girlsontherun.org/.
Go Far: healthy lifestyle choices for children.
www.gofarclub.org/.
Fleet Feet Kids Programs.
Kids: www.fleetfeetsports.com/training-programs/kids.
Boulder: www.fleetfeetboulder.com/mountainlionskidstraining.

Find Running Clubs in Your Area

Australia: Little Athletics Australia.
  www.littleathletics.com.au/.
Colorado: Landsharks.
  landsharkrunclub.com/.
New York: Young Runners (NYRR).
  www.nyrr.org/youth-and-schools/young-runners.
Oregon: Beaverton Youth Track Club.
  www.beavertonyouthtrack.com/.
United States: USATF—Club Search.
  www.usatf.org/clubs/search/.

RUNNING FORM VIDEOS

B. M. (director). *Essentials of Running Mechanics with Bobby McGee*. 2011 September 27. www.youtube.com/watch?v=GSGzqkjrWRA.
B. M. (director). *Running Warm-up Drills: Hamstring Extensions and Series*. www.youtube.com/watch?v=vZhNbNNnF5E&list=PL8E2JaqJ8WPflzj9zNRLQ2tU9tLMxFjRG.

RUNNING SHOES AND ATTIRE

Boulder Running Company—JackRabbit.
  www.jackrabbit.com/info/boulder-running-company.
Flatirons Running Inc: Boulder's finest, locally owned, full-service running store.
  www.flatironsrunning.com/.
Fleet Feet Sports.
  www.fleetfeetsports.com/.
Running Warehouse: your one-stop online retailer for everything running.
  www.runningwarehouse.com/.
Roadrunner Sports: the world's largest running store.
  www.roadrunnersports.com/.

INDEX

Achilles tendonitis, 73, 85
advanced runner schedules, *21–23*
Advil, 76
agility, 15, 90
aging, 8–9, 114, 117–18, 121–23,
    125–26
Aleve, 76
Alexander, Craig, 36
Alexander, Lucy, 5–6, 36, 100, 106–7
Alexander, Neirda, 106
amenorrhea, 50
anemia, 45–46, 54
ankle springs, 118
ankle stretches, 83
ankling, 118
anorexia, 48–51
antioxidants, 45
arm circles, 18
arm pullbacks, 119
arm stretches, 116
athlete feedback, 33–34
athletic bras, 26, 31
Atkins, Robert, 53
Atkins diet, 53

attitude, 94–97, 99
Australia, 5–6

B12 (vitamin), 45, 54
back stretches, 116
backward skipping, 119
Balyi, Istvan, 12
Bean, Gavin, 38
Bean, Marist, 38
Bean, Wrenn, 37–38
beanbag races, 41
Bearak, Barry, 61
Beck, Kevin, 25, 42, 51
beginner runner schedules, *20–22*
body basics, 11–19
body fat, 17
Bolder Boulder 10K, 106
bone development, 15–17, 50
Boulder Track Club, 106
Bowers, John, 106–7
boys. *See* men; youth running
bras, 26, 31
Brittin, Lize, 49–50, 60
Brown, Bruce E., 41

bulimia, 50–51
burnout. *See* psychology
butterfly game, 39–40
butt kicks, 19

calories, 44, 55
calve stretches, 116
camps, 103–5, 107–8
capture the flag, 40
carbohydrates, 44, 53, 55–56
children. *See* youth running
cholesterol, 45
chronic injuries, 69–70
clothing. *See* equipment
clubs, 104; Boulder Track Club, 106;
    Girls on the Run, 107; Heart and
    Soul, 107; Junior Olympics program,
    103, 107; Land Sharks, 105–6;
    Mountain Warriors, 106; psychology
    and, 108; seasonal teams as, 105–8;
    USA Track and Field, 103, 107; for
    youth running, 103, 105–8
coaching, 66; for attitude, 95–96;
    boundaries for, 42; in camps, 104;
    for clubs, 107–8; competition and,
    66–68; eating disorders and, 48–51;
    emotional support from, 35–36;
    families and, 49; feedback from,
    34–35; for form, 66–67; for goals,
    109–10, 112; improvement from, 14;
    injuries and, 62–63, 67, 69, 71, 78–
    79; nutrition and, 46–49; parenting
    and, 65; private, 65; psychology for,
    7, 61, 66–68, 94; recovery in, 123; in
    seasonal teams, 105; specialization
    and, 66–68; for strength, 16;
    training and, 7, 63–65, 67–68, 126;
    for women, 17, 49, 62–63; for youth
    running, 3, 6–8, 49, 62–66, 111–12,
    121–23
competition: attitude for, 95, 97;
    calories for, 55; in camps, 104;
    carbohydrates for, 55–56; coaching
    and, 66–68; families and, 33–34,
    41–42; goals for, 98; injuries and,

75; Ironman triathlon, 36; for
    LTAD, 13; nutrition for, 54–56;
    protein for, 55–56; psychology
    for, 93; for running, 111–12,
    126; sample meals for, 57–58;
    in seasonal teams, 105; self-talk
    for, 100–101; spikes for, 27;
    visualization for, 98–99; for youth
    running, 112, 118, 121, 126
complementary training, 90–91
cross-country running, 1, 9, 91, 103, 122
crossovers, 19
cross-training: ankle stretches for,
    83; clamshells, 83; cross-country
    ski machines for, 91; elliptical
    trainers for, 91; glute bridges,
    84; hip rotations, 82–84; for
    injuries, 75, 81–82; iron cross, 84;
    mobility exercises for, 82–85; pool
    running for, 91; quadruped hip
    extension with knee bent, 83; for
    rehabilitation, 85–86; side leg lifts,
    83; squats for, 84–85; stationary
    bikes for, 91; strength from, 86–89,
    92; in training, 75, 81, 89–91; for
    youth running, 90–91
crunches, 88
Culpepper, Alan, 68
Culpepper, Shayne, 68
Culpepper Mill, 68

dead lifts, 88
DeVinny, Alexandra, 49
dieting, 52–54
distance running, 1, 3, 52, 109–11, 122;
    marathons for, 36, 106, 114
drills, 18–19, 118–20

eating disorders, *51*, 52; anorexia, 48–
    51; bulimia, 50–51; coaching and,
    48–51; female athlete triad, 16–17,
    50; nutrition and, 43, 46–51, 59;
    parenting and, 62–63
elliptical trainers, 91
emotional support, 33, 35–36

endurance. *See* strength
England, 9
equipment, 113; bras, 26, 31; foam
    rollers, 29, 75; footwear, 26–27;
    Gore-Tex, 30; GPS for, 25, 27–28;
    heart rate monitors, 28; inserts,
    for shoes, 26; for night running,
    30–31; online training logs, 28; for
    recovery, 29–30, 75; Roll Recovery
    R8, 29; running shoes, 26–27, 31–
    32; for safety, 30–31; The Stick, 29;
    for training, 27–29; watches, 27–28;
    for water, 28–29; for winter, 30; for
    women, 31–32; YakTrax, 30
erythropoietin, 123
Eyestone, Ed, 82

Fairchild, Melody, 63–65, 68, 125–26
families, 49, 51; competition and, 33–
    34, 41–42; emotional support from,
    33, 35–36; fun with, 37–38; games
    for, 38–41
fat, 17
fat (in food), 44–45, 53
fatigue, 94
feedback, 33–35
female athlete triad, 16–17, 50
females. *See* women
fevers, 77
finances, 113
Fitbit, 25
fitness, 5
flashlights, 31
Fleshman, Lauren, 68
foam rollers, 29, 75
footwear, 26–27
form, 66–67, 70, 72–73
Fry, Scott, 67–68

gait analysis, 26
games, 37–41, 118
Garmin, 25
gear. *See* equipment
girls. *See* women; youth running
Girls on the Run (club), 107

global positioning satellite (GPS), 25,
    27–28
glute bridges, 84
glute stretches, 116–17
goals: attitude and, 94–95; coaching
    for, 109–10, 112; in psychology, 97–
    98; for training, 98, 114; for youth
    running, 111–12, 114
Google Maps, 25
Gore-Tex, 30
GPS. *See* global positioning satellite
groin stretches, 115

hamstring stretches, 115
Hansen, Richey, 7, 70–71, 73–74
health. *See* injuries
Heart and Soul (club), 107
heart rate, 28, 91–92
Higdon, Hal, 117
Higgins, Barb, 62, 64, 67, 117–18
high-fructose corn syrup, 43–44
hip rotations, 82–84
Hudson, Brad, 25; on injuries, 77–78;
    on psychology, 94, 96; schedules by,
    18–19, *20–23*; on youth running,
    4–5, 8–9, 33

iliotibial band syndrome, 73–74
illness, 76–77
Infeld, Emily, 91
influenza, 77
injuries, 108; Achilles tendonitis, 73, 85;
    Advil for, 76; Aleve for, 76; anemia
    as, 45–46, 54; anorexia as, 48–51;
    bone development and, 15–16;
    chronic, 69–70; coaching and, 62–63,
    67, 69, 71, 78–79; competition and,
    75; cross-training for, 75, 81–82;
    feedback for, 35; fevers as, 77; form
    and, 72–73; gait analysis for, 26;
    iliotibial band syndrome, 73–74;
    influenza as, 77; micro-tears, 72;
    nutrition and, 47, 74, *74*; physical
    therapy for, 76; plantar fasciitis, 72–
    73; psychology of, 78–79; recovery

for, 74–75, 75; rehabilitation for, 85–86; runner's knee, 72; shin splints, 70–71; sprains, 72; strains, 72; strength and, 16, 72, 74, 78, 85–86; stress fractures, 71–72, 76; training and, 71, 77–78; walking boot for, 73; youth running and, 14–15, 69–70, 74–75

inserts, for shoes, 26

intermediate runner schedules, 20–21, 23

iron, 54

Ironman triathlon, 36

Japan, 5

jogging, 26, 77

journaling, 96

Junior Olympics program (club), 103, 107

Kennedy, Christine, 117

Kenya, 3

Keto diet, 53

kids. See youth running

Land Sharks (club), 61, 105–6

leg curls, 87–88

leg swings, 120

logs, 28–29

Long Term Athlete Development model (LTAD), 12–14

lunges, 119

macronutrients, 44–45

Magical Running (McGee), 122

males. See men

mantras, 99–100, 100

maps, 25

marathons. See distance running

maturation, 11–12, 45–46

McGee, Bobby, 50, 122

McGettigan-Dumas, Róisín, 8–9

medial tibial stress, 70–71

men, 11–12, 51

mental development, 13

mentors. See coaching

micro-tears, 72

Miller, Rob, 41

minerals, 45–46

Moller, Lorraine, 6, 99–100

motivation, 37, 98, 110

Mountain Warriors (club), 106

muscles. See strength

music, 31

New Zealand, 6

night running, 30–31

nutrition, x, 57–58; for bone development, 15; coaching and, 46–49; for competition, 54–56; dieting and, 52–54; fat and, 44–45, 53; female athlete triad and, 16–17, 50; high-fructose corn syrup and, 43–44; injuries and, 47, 74, 74; macronutrients for, 44–45; nutrition bars, 29; protein for, 44–45, 54–56; psychology and, 47–49; for training, 47–48, 55; vitamins for, 45–46, 54; for youth running, 44, 46–49. See also eating disorders

obstacle courses, 41

older runners. See aging

Olympics, 8, 99, 113–14

online training logs, 28

Paleo diet, 53

parenting: for attitude, 95–96; clubs and, 103, 107–8; coaching and, 65; eating disorders and, 62–63; psychology for, 62–63, 94. See also families

patience, 13–14, 73, 78–79, 85, 94

physical therapy, 4, 7, 76

physiology, 11, 16–17

piriformis, 115

Plaatjes, Mark, 3–4

planks, 86

plantar fasciitis, 72–73

plyometrics, 15

pool running, 91
pressure. *See* psychology
private coaching, 65
protein, 44–45, 54–56
psoas stretches, 115
psychology, 41–42; attitude in, 94–97; clubs and, 108; for coaching, 7, 61, 66–68, 94; for competition, 93; of distance running, 52; emotional support and, 33, 35–36; families and, 33–34; of fatigue, 94; feedback for, 33–34; fun and, 37–38; goals in, 97–98; of injuries, 78–79; of mantras, 99–100, *100*; motivation in, 37, 98, 110; nutrition and, 47–49; for parenting, 62–63, 94; for running, 3–5, 93–94, 103–4, 125–26; in seasonal teams, 105–6; self-talk in, 100–101; of success, 94; training and, 6, 64, 93–94; visualization in, 98–99; for youth running, 4, 6–9, 95, 121, 125–26. *See also* eating disorders
puberty, 11–12, 45–46
push-ups, 87

quadriceps stretches, 114–15

recovery, 27–28, 117; equipment for, 29–30, 75; for injuries, 74–75, 75; for youth running, 29, 121–23
rehabilitation, 85–86
rest days, 75
De Reuck, Colleen, 106
Roll Recovery R8, 29
routines, 96
runner's knee, 72
running, x; agility for, 15, 90; aging and, 114, 117–18; calories and, 44; carbohydrates for, 53, 55–56; climate and, 2; clubs for, 103–8; competition for, 111–12, 126; families and, 33–42; finances for, 113; games for, 37–41; maps for, 25; at night, 30–31; plyometrics for, 15; protein for, 55–56; psychology for, 3–5, 93–94, 103–4, 125–26; scholarships for, 2–4, 113; seasonal teams for, 105–8; specialization for, 12–13, 66–68, 110; speed for, 110–11; sprinting, 27, 109–11; strength for, 110–11; stretching for, 114–17; swimming and, 6; watches for, 27–28; for women, 113–14. *See also* cross-country running; distance running; equipment; track and field; training; youth running
running shoes, 26–27, 31–32

safety, 30–31
scavenger hunts, 37, 39, 118
schedules for training, 18–19, *20–23*
scholarships, 2–4, 113
seasonal teams, 105–8
self-talk, 100–101
shin splints, 70–71
Shorter, Frank, 114
side stretches, 117
skills, 109–10
South Africa, 3–4
specialization, 12–13, 66–68, 110
speed, 110–11
spikes, 27
sports bras, 26, 31
sprains, 72
sprinting, 27, 109–11
squats, 84–85
stationary bikes, 91
The Stick, 29
strains, 72
strength: cross-training for, 86–89, 92; for distance running, 52; injuries and, 16, 72, 74, 78, 85–86; for youth running, 16, 90, 110–11
stress fractures, 71–72, 76
stretching, 114–17
student athletes, 2
supplementary training, 89–90
swimming, 6

teams, 95

technology. *See* equipment

"The Thin Men" (Beck), 51

3,000-meter steeplechase, 8

toe raisers, 87

"Too Fast, Too Soon" (Bearak), 61

track and field, 7, 9, 14, 93–94, 109

training: for aging, 117–18; attitude for, 95, 97; calories for, 55; camps for, 104; coaching and, 7, 63–65, 67–68, 126; complementary training, 90–91; drills for, 18–19, 118–20; equipment for, 27–29; goals for, 98, 114; injuries and, 71, 77–78; logs for, 28–29; microcycles for, 121; nutrition for, 47–48, 55; online training logs for, 28; overtraining, 17; psychology and, 6, 64, 93–94; schedules for, 18–19, *20–23*; for speed, 111; for strength, 16, 111; supplementary training, 89–90; in United States, 18; visualization in, 99; for youth running, 2, 5–6, 8, 109, 121–23. *See also* cross-training

Training on Empty (Brittin), 49–50

Umberger, Rachel, 62

United States, 1–5, 7, 18, 103, 107

veganism, 53–54

vegetarianism, 53–54

visualization, 98–99

vitamins, 45–46, 54

VO2Max, 17, 50, 114

Walker, Ariel, 34, 37

Walker, Rebecca, 34, 37

walking boot, 73

Waller, Ruth, 9

watches, 27–28

Weich, Greg, 27

Welsch, Heather, 61

Welsch, Kaytlynn, 61

Welsch, Rodney, 61

Winfrey, Oprah, 114

winter gear, 30

women: anemia in, 45–46, 54; coaching for, 17, 49, 62–63; equipment for, 31–32; female athlete triad for, 16–17, 50; Girls on the Run for, 107; Heart and Soul for, 107; maturation for, 11; running for, 113–14. *See also* eating disorders

Wrenn, Bean, 105–6, 118

Wrenn, Marist, 106

YakTrax, 30

Yankovic, Weird Al, 43

youth running, 35; aging and, 8–9, 117–18, 121–23, 125–26; attitude for, 95–97; bone development in, 15–16; camps for, 103–5; clubs for, 103, 105–8; coaching for, 3, 6–8, 49, 62–66, 111–12, 121–23; competition for, 112, 118, 121, 126; cross-country for, 122; cross-training for, 90–91; for distance, 122; education for, 7; emotional support for, 36; female athlete triad in, 16–17; fun and, 37–38; games for, 37–41; goals for, 111–12, 114; injuries and, 14–15, 69–70, 74–75; Land Sharks (club) for, 61, 105–6; maturation and, 11–12; at night, 30–31; nutrition for, 44, 46–49; psychology for, 4, 6–9, 95, 121, 125–26; recovery for, 29, 121–23; schedules for, 18–19, *20–23*; skills for, 109–10; speed for, 110–11; strength for, 16, 90, 110–11; stress fractures for, 71; training for, 2, 5–6, 8, 109, 121–23; visualization for, 98–99. *See also* eating disorders; equipment

ABOUT THE AUTHORS

Brad Hudson and Kevin Beck are both well-established, extremely active, and well-known figures in the running community. Both now live in Boulder, Colorado, but have worked extensively with kids and adults alike in various parts of the country from coast to coast.

Brad Hudson is one of the most respected distance-running coaches in the United States. He is the co-author, along with Matt Fitzgerald, of the 2008 book *How to Run Faster from 5K to the Marathon* (www.amazon.com/gp/product/0767928229), which as of January 2015 had sold more than 41,000 copies. Brad competed in the Olympic Trials Marathon himself, training and racing beginning at the age of ten under current and legendary University of Colorado coach Mark Wetmore. His 2:17:03 marathon in Chicago in 1985 at age nineteen remains one of the fastest times ever recorded by a junior U.S. athlete. He has coached a slew of world-class runners in Eugene, Oregon, and Boulder, including Olympian Dathan Ritzenhein and U.S. half-marathon champion James Carney. In 2012, eleven of his athletes qualified for the U.S. Olympic Trials Marathon in Houston, a total already exceeded for the 2016 Trials in Los Angeles. He is the founder of Marathon Performance (www.marathonperformance.com/) and is now the head of the burgeoning Boulder Valley–based Hudson Training Systems Elite group (htselite.org/). His athletes excel not only at the marathon but in cross-country and track and field as well.

Brad's training expertise is in continual demand. He has spoken regularly at a wide variety of functions around the country, ranging from summer clinics hosted by the Cross-Country Coaches Association of Texas to talks at Powell's Bookstore in Portland, Oregon. He has delivered talks at the Eugene Marathon pre-race expo, at Jay Johnson's renowned cross-country and track camp in Colorado, at Scott Simmons's Distance Summit in Charlotte, North Carolina, and at the Boulder Center for Sports Medicine. He has been an integral part of seminars at the Oregon Track Club Masters Clinic and in 2014 branched out to address triathletes at a clinic in Washington, D.C. He has been interviewed a number of times by FloTrack.com, the premier online repository for live top-level track and field webcasts and race results (www.flotrack.org/coverage/248438-2012-Outdoor-Track-and -Field-Season/video/635265-Brad-Hudson-answers-questions-talks-Hudson -Training-Systems-in-Spring-2012), and by the New York Road Runners.

Kevin Beck, a native of Concord, New Hampshire, has been running for close to thirty years and writing professionally about the sport since 1999, with more than one hundred articles to his credit. Kevin edited the 2005 book *Run Strong*, which has sold more than 11,000 copies and has garnered numerous positive reviews (www.humankinetics.com/products/all-products/ run-strong). Publications featuring his work include *Running Times* (where Kevin was a senior writer for more than a dozen years—www.runnersworld .com/rt-miscellaneous/kevin-beck), *Competitor Running, Marathon & Beyond, Men's Fitness, the Roanoke Valley Sports Journal, Triathlete Magazine,* the New York Road Runners, *Florida Running and Triathlon, Level Renner, Parks and Recreation,* the *Roanoker,* and more. He has coached at the high-school and open-category levels and given talks and clinics at venues ranging from large pre-marathon dinner gatherings—for example, at the Space Coast Marathon in 2005—to groups of the Boy Scouts of America. He has been regularly interviewed in print and via podcasts and online radio broadcasts over the years. Since June of 2013 alone, he has written more than thirty articles for *Running Times, Competitor Running,* and *Level Runner* alone. Along with two-time U.S. Olympian Pete Pfitzinger, he founded a coaching website in 2002, DistanceCoach.com, and remains highly active in an online-coaching capacity (www.kemibe.com). He has been interviewed by New Hampshire Public Radio (kemibe.com/beck.mp3) and by Bart Yasso of Pure Fit Radio (watersportnews.com/news/story/111112/episode-24/full_story.html) and was featured in an article by Pete Pfitzinger in *Running Times,* "Chasing the Dream" (www.runnersworld.com/elite-runners/chasing-dream-1?page=4). He was the subject of Jonathan Beverly's "Editor's Note" in the May 2005 issue of *Running Times* as a result of his contributions to the magazine over the years as well as his personal running accomplishments. FluidRunning.com founder Jennifer Conroyd credits Kevin's wisdom about deep-water running (www.dailyherald.com/article/20130325/news/703259847) with largely inspiring her now-popular business (www.fluidrunning.com).

Kevin has been consulted by a variety of journalists for running-related articles, including Matt Fitzgerald's "Take a Shortcut" for Runner's World (www.runnersworld.com/running-tips/take-shortcut), "Train for Speed" in the Allentown (Pa.) *Morning Call*, and "Running Safely into Middle Age" in Bloomberg *BusinessWeek* (www.bloomberg.com/bw/stories/2007-05-20/running-safely-into-middle-age). He took part in a 2008 podcast hosted by Scott Douglas, now a senior content editor for *Runner's World*, in which he discussed his experiences training with soon-to-be-Olympians Shannon Rowbury and Erin Donohue in Sarasota, Florida (www.runnersworld.com/race-training/rt-radio-interview-illustrious-and-elusive-kevin-beck).

As a coach of young runners, Kevin achieved considerable success in a short time. At Bishop Brady High School in New Hampshire, beginning with a boys' team in 1999 that had finished eighteenth out of twenty-one teams in the Class I State Meet. Kevin led a team consisting of eight runners in 1999 to a twelfth-place state-meet finish, and the next year Bishop Brady took fourth, giving the Green Giants their first berth in the New Hampshire Cross-Country Meet of Champions in school history. Kevin built a website for the team along the way (kemibe.com/bbxc/index.htm) and wrote about his coaching experiences for *Running Times* in "They Might Be Giants" (www.runnersworld.com/high-school/they-might-be-giants).

As an athlete, Kevin was a multi-time all-state selection in high school and ran all of his personal bests in his thirties, including 51:32 for ten miles, 1:08:29 for the half-marathon, and 2:24:17 for the marathon.

Lize Brittin, a lifelong resident of Boulder, Colorado, and a writer since 2001, is the author of *Training on Empty* and has written for a variety of publications, including *Competitor Running*, *Active Cities*, *Boulder Magazine*, and *Thrill*. She holds a bachelor of arts in psychology from the University of Colorado. As a high-schooler, she was a three-time Colorado state cross-country and track champion and qualified twice for the Kinney (now Foot Locker) National Cross-Country Championship after winning the Kinney Midwest Regionals as a senior. At age sixteen, she set a women's record at the Pikes Peak Ascent, considered one of the most challenging mountain races in the country.